The 21st Century Workforce:

HANDBOOK FOR MANAGING TELEWORKERS

TOOLKIT

By
Sandra Gurvis & Don Philpott

Published by
Government Training Inc.™
ISBN: 978-0-9844038-8-2

About the Publisher – Government Training Inc. ™

Government Training Inc. provides worldwide training, publishing and consulting to government agencies and contractors that support government in areas of business and financial management, acquisition and contracting, physical and cyber security, intelligence operations and grant writing. Our management team and instructors are seasoned executives with demonstrated experience in areas of Federal, State, Local and DoD needs and mandates.

Recent books published by Government Training Inc. ™ include:

☐ The COTR Handbook
☐ Performance Based Contracting Handbook
☐ The Grant Writer's Handbook
☐ The Integrated Physical Security Handbook
☐ Handbook for Managing Teleworkers
☐ Small Business Guide to Government Contracting
☐ Cost Reimbursable Contracting
☐ Securing Our Schools
☐ Workplace Violence

For more information on the company, its publications and professional training, go to www.GovernmentTrainingInc.com.

Copyright © 2010 Government Training Inc. All rights reserved.

Printed in the United States of America.

This publication is protected by copyright, and permission must be obtained from the publisher prior to any prohibited reproduction, storage in a retrieval system or transmission in any form or by any means, electronic, mechanical, photocopying, recording or likewise. For information regarding permissions, write to:

Government Training Inc. ™
Rights and Contracts Department
5372 Sandhamn Place
Longboat Key, Florida 34228
don.dickson@GovernmentTrainingInc.com

ISBN: 978-0-9844038-8-2

Sources:

This book has drawn heavily on the authoritative materials published by a wide range of sources.

These materials are in the public domain, but accreditation has been given both in the text and in the reference section if you need additional information.

The author and publisher have taken great care in the preparation of this handbook, but make no expressed or implied warranty of any kind and assume no responsibility for errors or omissions.

No liability is assumed for incidental or consequential damages in connection with or arising out of the use of the information or recommendations contained herein.

We also wish to thank the Telework Exchange for their permission to quote from their telework content. (www.teleworkexchange.com)

Handbook for Managing Teleworkers – Toolkit

CONTENTS

Introduction 1

Overview: Telework in Today's Government 3

Step One. Overcoming Management Resistance 15
   The Arguments For Teleworking 15
      Continuity of Operations 15
      Reduction of Energy Consumption and the Associated Carbon Footprint 17
      Improved Performance 18
      Greater Flexibility, Morale, and Decreased Stress 20
      Improved Recruitment, Retention, and Staffing 21
      Improved Accommodations for Persons with Disabilities 22
      Flexible Dependent Care 23
      Office Space and Operating Cost Savings 23
      Optimal Use of Technological Advances 24
   Q & A: What About Me – The Manager? 29
   Success Stories 44

Step Two. Choosing Employees for Telework 49
   Selection Criteria 51
   Success Stories 68

Step Three. Training Managers and Teleworkers 75
   A Program That Works For Everyone 75
   Maintain Harmony in the Office 76
   Acknowledge Your Employees' Achievements 77
   Training Managers 77
   Feedback For Telecommuters 81
   Telework Pitfalls 82
   Training Teleworkers 84
   Success Stories 88

Step Four. Motivation: Developing and Building Trust and Mentoring 95
   Coaching and Counseling 99
   Coaching vs. Counseling 100
   Success Stories 110

Handbook for Managing Teleworkers – Toolkit

Step Five. Virtual Teams and Change Management 117
Developing The Team.. 117
Change Management.. 121
The Four Dynamics of Change 122
Change and Emotional Intelligence 126
Success Story.. 126

Appendix 1 131
Benefits of Telework 131

Appendix 2 145
Federal Management Regulation; Guidelines for Alternative Workplace Arrangements 145

Appendix 3 155
*Information Technology and Telecommunications Guidelines for Federal Telework and
Other Alternative Workplace Arrangement Programs General Services Administration* 155

Appendix 4 167
Department of Justice Telework Program Agreement 167

Appendix 5 171
From Work to Telework – Small and Smart Mobile Solutions 171

Appendix 6... 183
Presidential Directive... 183

About the authors

Sandra Gurvis

Sandra Gurvis (www.sgurvis.com), professional development instructor for Government Training Inc (GTI), is the author of fifteen books and hundreds of magazine articles. Her titles include MANAGING THE TELECOMMUTING EMPLOYEE with Michael Amigoni (Adams, 2009), MANAGEMENT BASICS, 2nd ed (Adams, 2007), and CAREER FOR CONFORMISTS (Marlowe, 2001), which was a selection of the Quality Paperback Book Club. Her books have been featured on "Good Morning America," "CBS Up to the Minute," "ABC World News Tonight," in USA Today and in other newspapers and on television and radio stations across the country; and have been excerpted in magazines.

Sandra has traveled throughout the US, lecturing and providing information on telework and telecommuting, as well as other issues relating to management and self-employment. She lives in Columbus, Ohio.

She is also the author of HANDBOOK FOR MANAGING TELEWORKERS published by Government Training Inc.

Don Philpott

Don Philpott is editor of International Homeland Security, a quarterly journal for homeland security professionals, and has been writing, reporting and broadcasting on international events, trouble spots and major news stories for more than 40 years. For 20 years he was a senior correspondent with Press Association -Reuters, the wire service, and traveled the world on assignments including Northern Ireland, Lebanon, Israel, South Africa and Asia.

He writes for magazines and newspapers in the United States and Europe and is a contributor to radio and television programs on security and other issues. He is the author of more than 90 books on a wide range of subjects and has had more than 5,000 articles printed in publications around the world. His most recent books are Terror - Is America Safe?, The Wounded Warrior Handbook, The Workplace Violence Prevention Handbook, and Public School Emergency Preparedness and Crisis Management. He is a member of the National Press Club.

Symbols

Throughout this book you will see a number of icons displayed in the margins. The icons are there to help you as you work through the Five Step process. Each icon acts as an advisory – for instance alerting you to things that you must always do or should never do. The icons used are:

 Must Do — This is something that you must always do

 No No — This is something you should never do

Tips — Really useful tips

 Remember — Points to bear in mind

 Checklist — Have you checked off or answered everything on this list?

Handbook for Managing Teleworkers – Toolkit

Additional Handbooks Published by Government Training Inc.
For details, go to www.GovernmentTrainingInc.com

The COTR Handbook

Performance-Based Contracting

Managing Cost Reimbursable Contracts

Handbook for Managing Teleworkers

Small Business Contracting

Workplace Violence

Grant Writer's Handbook

Protecting Our Schools

The Integrated Physical Security Handbook

Handbook for Managing Teleworkers – Toolkit

INTRODUCTION

Telework is coming and nowhere is this truer than in the Federal government. In today's world, employees are no longer content to stay locked in the traditional 9 to 5 jobs. With the improvements in technology, employees now look for increased job flexibility, which provides a better work-life balance.

The Federal government, however, has an equally important reason for encouraging telework. The two devastating blizzards in Washington D.C. in January 2010 almost closed down the government because hundreds of thousands were unable to get into work. Had those employees been working from home, government functions could have continued uninterrupted. Teleworking is one way to ensure continuation of government operations in the event of a major disaster or terrorist attack.

Recent Presidential directives promote teleworking and urge Federal departments to do more to encourage and implement it – not as a privilege but as a right. Most surveys show that Federal workers want to telework and would welcome the chance to participate.

The American Federation of Government Employees (AFGE) is the largest Federal employee union representing 600,000 Federal and D.C. government workers nationwide and overseas. It fully supports teleworking and has agreements in place with many Federal departments – most recently HUD – which protect the rights of its members.

One of the biggest stumbling blocks to implementation, however, is reluctance on the part of many senior managers. There are still strongly felt beliefs that employees working at home will be less productive and that somehow, their position, as manager will be diminished. In fact, nothing could be further from the truth.

Survey after survey show that teleworkers are as productive and in many cases more so than their office colleagues. The findings also show that the most efficient teleworkers are those who are properly managed.

Government departments must have a joint focus – encouraging more people to telework and ensuring that managers overseeing teleworkers are properly trained. This also means providing the best tools to support and manage telework teams.

www.GovernmentTrainingInc.com

Handbook for Managing Teleworkers – Toolkit

HANDBOOK FOR MANAGING TELEWORKERS TOOLKIT aims to show you how to do that. It is an easy to understand five-step process that will guide you towards understanding and working with teleworkers by choosing, motivating, and training the best people; developing trust and mentoring; working with virtual teams and dealing with change in the work environment. The book contains best practices and real-life cases studies from Federal departments and agencies. Along with practical tips, information, and checklists, it also contains samples of teleworking agreements and other documents needed to implement a telework program.

Overview: Telework in Today's Government

The most recent data from OPM show that although 62 percent of Federal employees are eligible to work remotely, less than 6 percent of all full-time Federal workers telework even one day a month.

Remember

Table 1 Eligible employees who teleworked in the federal government in 2008

Agency	# of Eligible Employees	% of Eligible Employees Teleworking	Teleworking 1-2 Days/Week	Teleworking 3 Days/Week
Patent and Trademark Office	5,314	82.7	46.1	36.6
General Services Administration	10,374	45.8	39.7	2.3
Securities and Exchange Commission	3,671	43.5	12.8	2.9
National Science Foundation	1,438	41.0	12.6	0.5
Office of Personnel Management	2,357	34.2	18.6	7.5
Environmental Protection Agency	16,337	32.1	19.6	<0.1
Department of Transportation	22,528	29.8	8.5	3.9
Federal Deposit Insurance Corporation	5,194	27.4	6.1	1.3
Federal Energy Regulatory Commission	1,417	24.0	16.8	0.0
Department of Housing and Urban Development	8,100	23.8	19.2	2.8
Department of Interior	45,319	23.7	11.9	3.7
Social Security Administration	14,557	23.6	19.7	1.7
Department of Health and Human Services	59,158	21.6	12.5	1.0
Department of Veterans Affairs	20,455	20.3	6.4	6.6
Department of Education	3,825	10.4	8.3	1.2
Department of Labor	15,136	10.4	35.2	1.0
Department of Commerce	35,130	8.5	44.5	0.2
Department of State	14,207	7.1	3.0	0.3
Department of Agriculture	87,432	6.4	2.4	0.6
Department of Energy	13,231	5.7	2.7	0.3
Department of the Treasury	96,652	5.6	2.5	1.5

Handbook for Managing Teleworkers – Toolkit

Agency	# of Eligible Employees	% of Eligible Employees Teleworking	Teleworking 1-2 Days/Week	Teleworking 3 Days/Week
Department of Justice	37,023	4.7	2.1	1.3
National Aeronautics and Space Administration	18,224	4.5	1.5	0.7
Department of Defense	564,562	3.0	1.4	0.3
Department of Homeland Security	54,875	2.5	1.1	0.4

(Note: OPM's 2009 telework report did not include data from members of the Intelligence Community.)
Source: *Status of Telework in the Federal Government, 2009*

In 2007, Telework Exchange, Federal Managers Association (FMA), and TANDBERG released the study, titled "Face-to-Face with Management Reality - A Telework Research Report." Based on a survey of more than 200 government managers from 45 defense and civilian agencies, the report revealed that "Federal management resistance is a strong barrier to telework and highlights a perception that there is limited topdown support for telework. "

Remember: Survey results indicate that only 35 percent of Federal managers believe their agencies supported telework, despite a 2001 Congressional mandate that requires agencies to implement telework programs. However, the study demonstrated that attitudes toward telework improved dramatically as managers became more exposed to alternative work arrangements. Fifty-four percent of non-teleworking managers had favorable views of telework. That number jumped to 75 percent among managers who telework themselves.

The message was that more managers should try telework and understand its value.

Tips: Going beyond the statistics, the study suggested recommendations that would help to turn the tide on managers' attitudes and perceptions of telework. Manager-specific pilot programs are one way to address telework concerns. If managers can have a successful telework experience, they are more likely to consider alternative work arrangements and agree their employees could do the same, and with equal or greater productivity.

Enhancing educational efforts across government is another key component to expanding management perceptions of telework. The study showed a low awareness of telework's importance in Continuity of Operations (COOP) strategies, and that making managers aware of all of the benefits and rewards of telework is essential in achieving higher levels of acceptance and adoption. Another recommendation addressed managers' concerns about productivity. In general, managers who telework agreed that teleworkers are as productive as their in-office counterparts.

Tips: Managers must base their employees' performance on work output by implementing performance-based review processes.

Overview: Telework in Today's Government

A final suggestion for improving management's support for telework involved face time. Thirty-two percent of respondents cited lack of face-to-face contact as a communications barrier to expanded telework. More than 60 percent of managers said they had misinterpreted a colleague through e-mail communications. Given these factors, agencies should stress the need for periodic personal contact and implement technologies that allow for face-to-face communications from remote locations. This is one area where technology is available now that can immediately improve operations and communications between employees, managers, and customers.

Telework Milestones

For more than 20 years, Federal government officials have been discussing telework options, alternatives, and strategies. Only in the past five years have technology, traffic, and talent converged to make these concepts a reality for many government employees, managers, and their constituents.

2000

Congress passed Public Law 106-346. Each executive agency shall establish a policy under which eligible employees of the agency may participate in telecommuting to the maximum extent possible without diminished employee performance

2005

OPM reports that 119,000 Federal employees teleworked in 2005 with 60 percent of them teleworking at least once a week

Roughly 36,000 civilian Defense Department employees are due to be relocated over the next three years as part of the base realignment and closure, or BRAC, process. Agencies, like DISA, are use telework solutions to combat BRAC

Telework Exchange launched, providing a series of Telework value calculators that tally the cost of Federal commuting

2006

Virginia Governor Kaine signed an executive order establishing the Office of Telework Promotion and Broadband Assistance OPM reports that 110,592 employees are teleworking in the Federal government

2007

OPM reports that 94,643 Federal employees teleworked, representing 7.62 percent of all employees eligible to telework and the number of agencies that have fully integrated telework into emergency planning has increased from 42 to 60 percent in 2006. (Note, decrease in teleworking is a result of how agencies defined regular and reoccurring telework)

www.GovernmentTrainingInc.com

2008

A CDW survey shows that private sector telecommuting adoption is on the rise (14 percent) and catching up to the adoption rates of Federal employees (17 percent)

The Office of Personnel Management (OPM) reports that 102,900 employees are teleworking, representing 8.67 percent of all employees eligible to telework

2009

April

OPM Director, John Berry, announces five-part plan to increase participation in the Federal government's telework programs

August

Gov. Tim Kaine announced the first ever statewide Telework Day. Teleworkers saved approximately $113,000, avoided driving 14,000 miles, and removed 75.89 tons of pollutants from the air on this day

United States Patent and Trademark Office reported in their 2009 Telework Annual Report that to date more than 1,300 patent examiners have relinquished their office space to work from home four days per week. This has enabled the agency to avoid securing $11 million in additional office space

October

President Obama issued Executive Order 13514 that states that Federal agencies must reduce greenhouse gas emissions by 2020. Agencies need to evaluate employees' commuting profile and reduce its impact on the environment

December

In the next three years, public- and private-sector IT decision makers expect telework to increase by 65 percent and 33 percent, respectively

2010

January

The Administration is focused on three areas in telework: Business continuity, using telework to create jobs especially for Americans with disabilities, and reducing carbon footprints. OPM Director John Berry and Aneesh Chopra, the White House Chief Technical Officer, host a White House/Federal government group focused specifically on advancing telework in agencies

Overview: Telework in Today's Government

February

D.C. area hit with major snowstorm. OPM reported that the Federal government saved $30 million a day by teleworking

March

OPM Director John Berry states his goal to increase the number of eligible Federal employees who telework by 50 percent by FY 2011

The White House hosts a Forum on Workplace Flexibility. President Obama said the government is committed to leading by example

April

Feds urged to telework during D.C.'s Nuclear Summit

Telework Exchange hosts 7th Town Hall Meeting. White House promises more attention to Americans with disabilities and encourages telework

May

Senate passes The Telework Enhancement Act of 2010 (S. 707) which requires each executive agency to establish a telework policy, determine, and notify eligible employees, provide an interactive telework training program, and ensure that no distinction is made between teleworkers and nonteleworkers for purposes of performance appraisals, work requirements, or other acts involving managerial discretion

Representative James Moran predicts that commuting time in northern Virginia could increase to up to 5 hours per day when at least 13,000 BRAC jobs are relocated from Crystal City, which is two Metro stops from the Pentagon, to areas mostly dependent on cars. Forcing workers onto northern Virginia's roads will hinder their productivity.

OPM found was that 10 percent of its employees said they telework at least one day a week. That translates to 200,000 Federal employees, meaning more Federal workers are teleworking than OPM previously thought.

Source: Telework Exchange

September 2010

On September 30, the Senate approved a compromise federal teleworking bill. Under the Telework Improvements Act of 2010 (H.R. 1722), agencies will have 180 days to determine the eligibility of all employees to telework and to establish policies for eligible employees. After an employee is deemed eligible, he or she must enter into a written telework arrangement with the

Handbook for Managing Teleworkers – Toolkit

agency. Eligible feds could telework at least 20 percent of the hours they work each two-week period.

H.R. 1722 also requires agencies to incorporate telework into their continuity-of-operations plans, allowing them to head off the effects of events such as the blizzards that struck the Washington, D.C., area this year. The bill also orders the Office of Personnel Management to expand telework training opportunities for employees and managers. The House now has to act on the compromise.

"Employing telework on a government-wide scale constitutes a significant culture shift in the federal workforce," said Federal Managers Association National President Patricia Niehaus, whose organization supports the bill.

Niehaus said the change will require "an increased investment in managerial training to maintain employee engagement, monitor performance and promote cooperation when face-to-face."

"This is a very welcome development," said National Treasury Employees Union President Colleen Kelley, who applauded the bill's training provision. "The more managers and employees understand telework, the more the advantages become clear."

Federal Manager's Take On Telework

The telework bandwagon is on a roll, with Congress and the Obama Administration touting the flexible work tool as the next big innovation in government efficiency. Although the merits of telework are well documented, the task of implementing telework policies falls on Federal managers, and they have real, valid concerns that deserve greater attention, says Patricia Niehaus, President of the Federal Managers Association, which represents 200,000 managers, supervisors, and executives serving in today's Federal government.

Remember

Recent studies have cited management resistance as one of the most significant impediments to expanded telework adoption. Due to lack of direct experience with teleworkers, the hesitancy with which many managers approach telework is understandable but not insurmountable. As an organization representing these very managers, the Federal Managers Association is committed to realizing the benefits of telework while finding solutions to managers' legitimate concerns.

Tips

For many managers, apprehension centers on the fear that embracing telework entails a surrender of workforce control and a subsequent drop in productivity. Managers note that a lack of face-to-face collaboration with employees, coupled with the difficulty in effectively measuring output, contributes to their trepidation. Additionally, stories regarding managers' struggles to contact unresponsive employees engaged in telework exacerbate reservations.

8   www.GovernmentTrainingInc.com

Overview: Telework in Today's Government

Key to reversing managers' resistance is the understanding of what telework is and what it is not.

First and foremost, telework is a cost-effective means to bolster agencies' delivery of services to the public. Some agencies have already demonstrated that incorporating telework on a large scale can improve continuity-of-operations plans, sustaining the delivery of government services in the event of a natural disaster or terrorist attack, while simultaneously improving everyday output.

Remember

Additionally, as the demand among employees for a more secure work/life balance grows, telework can serve as a critical recruitment and retention resource, one the private sector has offered for years and with which the Federal government is forced to compete. Telework is not a benefit reserved only for privileged employees and should not be viewed as such.

Employing telework on a government-wide scale constitutes a significant culture shift in the Federal workforce, one that requires an increased investment in training to teach managers how to maintain employee engagement, monitor performance, and promote cooperation when face-to-face communication is restricted.

Establishing trust between managers and employees is critical, and that trust can only be established if managers understand how to clearly lay out goals and objectives and communicate effectively with employees outside the office. Managers must hold all of their employees accountable for achieving performance results, but a telework environment requires supervisors to possess expanded competencies to manage operations remotely.

Must Do

Agency leaders should avoid a one-size-fits-all approach to telework and instead pursue creation of pilot programs to test the applicability of telework in their respective departments. Not all positions in the Federal government are amenable to telework, as certain jobs require the employee's physical presence in the office.

No No

In addition, underperforming employees, or those who require more direct supervision, should not be allowed to work remotely without first improving their performance. Pilot programs enable managers and employees to engage in a "trial run" without committing to a permanent arrangement and better prepare agencies to establish clear guidelines and goals to facilitate formal implementation.

It is no surprise that interest in telework is on the rise. This flexible work tool undoubtedly provides many benefits — not only to those participating but also to the agency and the nation. However, the concerns and recommendations of managers and supervisors charged with executing programs must be taken into account to achieve success.

The bottom line is that telework is coming to an agency near you. By being ahead of the curve and embracing the concept now, managers will have a positive impact on the productivity and appeal of their agencies.

Laws and Regulations

In accordance with Section 359 of Public Law 106–346, effective October 23, 2000, each Executive agency must establish a policy under which eligible employees of the agency may participate in telecommuting to the maximum extent possible without diminished employee performance.

Public Law 104–52, Treasury, Postal Service, and General Government Appropriations Act, 1996, title VI, § 620 (November 19, 1995), 31 U.S.C. § 1348 note, provides as follows: "Notwithstanding any provisions of this or any other Act, during the fiscal year ending September 30, 1996, and hereafter, any department, division, bureau, or office may use funds appropriated by this or any other Act to install telephone lines, and necessary equipment, and to pay monthly charges, in any private residence or private apartment of any employee who has been authorized to work at home in accordance with guidelines issued by the Office of Personnel Management: Provided, That the head of the department, division, bureau, or office certifies that adequate safeguards against private misuse exist, and that the service is necessary for direct support of the agency's mission."

Public Law 107–347, The E-Government Act of 2002 (December 17, 2002), recognized the importance of information security to the economic and national security interests of the United States. Title III of the EGovernment Act, referred to therein as the Federal Information Security Management Act of 2002 (FISMA), emphasizes the need for organizations to develop, document, and implement an organization-wide program to provide security for the information systems that support its operations and assets.

GSA Federal Management Regulation (FMR) Bulletin 2006–B3—Guidelines for Alternative Workplace Arrangements, effective March 17, 2006, sets forth the parameters for establishing agency AWA programs.

On July 14, 2010 The Telework Improvements Act (HR1722) was passed by the House Oversight and Government Reform Committee.

The act allows government employees to telework at least two days every two weeks from their home or satellite offices that are regionally placed.

It requires each executive agency to establish a policy under which employees may be authorized to telework to the maximum extent possible without diminishing employee performance or agency operations. Specifies circumstances under which teleworking will not be required. Provides that an agency shall not be considered to be in compliance with telework requirements unless employees authorized are permitted to telework for at least 20 percent of the hours worked in every two administrative workweeks.

Overview: Telework in Today's Government

Requires agencies to:

- ☐ provide training to teleworkers; and
- ☐ ensure that no distinction is made between teleworkers and nonteleworkers for performance appraisal, training, and other specified purposes.

Requires OPM to:

- ☐ prescribe telework regulations;
- ☐ provide teleworking assistance and guidance to agencies;
- ☐ maintain a central, publicly available telework website, including regulations regarding telework and a confidential hotline and e-mail address to report abuse; and
- ☐ provide a summary of any such reports to the Comptroller General.

Requires each agency to designate a Telework Managing Officer who shall:

- ☐ serve as a resource on teleworking for its supervisors, managers, and employees; and
- ☐ ensure that employees are notified of grievance procedures for telework disputes.

Requires the Comptroller General to:

- ☐ establish a system for evaluating each agency's telework policy and employee participation; and
- ☐ report annually to specified congressional committees on agency telework policies, participation, and practices. Sets forth provisions concerning incorporating teleworking into agency continuity of operations planning.

On July 26, 2010 President Obama issued an Executive Order ordering Federal agencies to increase employment of people with disabilities many of whom would be suitable for teleworking and the Office of Personnel Management (OPM) has announced it wants to see a significant telework increase by Fiscal Year 2011. The 2010 Federal Employee Viewpoint Survey revealed 64 percent of Federal workers could work remotely if given the opportunity, but only 10 percent currently telework at least once a week.

2010 Federal Employee Viewpoint Survey Results

The OPM conducted the 2010 Federal Employee Viewpoint Survey (FedView) Government-wide during February and March 2010. This was the fifth time OPM has conducted a survey of Federal employees. It previously ran the survey under the name Federal Human Capital Survey in 2002, 2004, 2006, and 2008.

Overall, FedView focuses on employee perceptions regarding critical areas of their work life, areas which drive employee satisfaction, commitment, and ultimately retention in the workforce,

Handbook for Managing Teleworkers – Toolkit

at a government-wide and agency-specific level. It is used to guide human resource management strategies and practices, providing essential feedback on agency trends to allow senior leaders to set directions or guide further improvements. Additionally, it incorporates the Human Capital Assessment and Accountability Framework, whose five human capital systems define the standards and metrics for effective human capital management in the Federal government.

The re-branded survey included new questions on work/life balance, and reorganized survey questions into new areas centered on the topics of work experience, work unit, agency, supervisor/team leader, leadership, and job satisfaction. The United States Agency for International Development (USAID) will be incorporating employee feedback from the survey as it creates and revises strategies, policies, and services to ensure the organization has the human capital environment needed to help employees complete their job's duties and enable USAID to accomplish its mission. This requires getting the right people in the right place, doing the right work, with the right skills, at the right time to pursue U.S. national interests abroad. USAID's success depends on the talent and motivation of its workforce. Recruiting and retaining the best and the brightest individuals depend, in large part, on the quality of the work environment.

Your Agency's Telework Situation

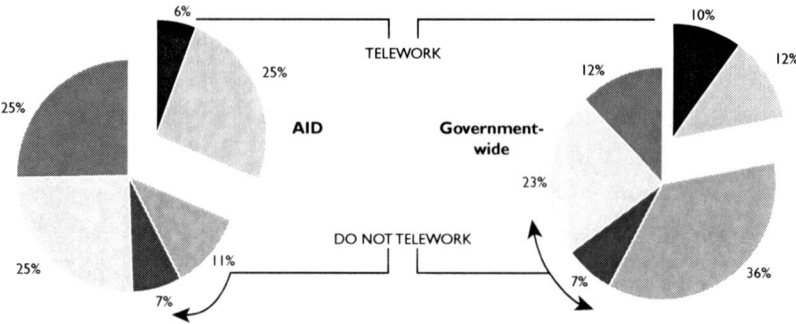

- ■ I telework on a regular basis (at least one entire work day a week).
- I telework infrequently (less than one entire work day a week).
- I DO NOT telework because I have to be physically present on the job (e.g., Law enforcement offcers, park rangers, security personnel).
- ■ I DO NOT telework because I have technical issues (e.g., Connectivity, inadequate equipment) that prevent me from teleworking.
- I DO NOT telework because I am not allowed to, even though I have the kind of job where I can telework.
- ■ I DO NOT telework because I choose not to telework.

Overview: Telework in Today's Government

How Satisfied Are You With The Following Worklife Programs In Your Agency?

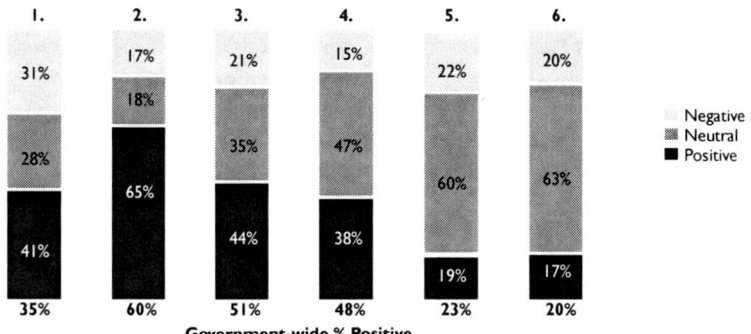

1. Telework (Not including 528 No Basis to Judge responses)
2. Alternative work schedules (Not including 353 No Basis to Judge responses)
3. Health and wellness programs (Not including 211 No Basis to Judge responses)
4. Employee assistance program (Not including 377 No Basis to Judge responses)
5. Child care programs (Not including 478 No Basis to Judge responses)
6. Elder care programs (Not including 487 No Basis to Judge responses)

Source: www.teleworkexchange.com

The Unions

The American Federation of Government Employees (AFGE) is the largest Federal employee union representing 600,000 Federal and D.C. government workers nationwide and overseas. It is a strong advocate of teleworking but believes that teleworkers rights to union representation need to be better protected.

In the 110th Congress, two bills addressed the issue of telework. The Telework Enhancement Act of 2007 (S. 1000) was reported out of the Committee on Homeland Security and Governmental Affairs in November 2007. The Telework Improvements Act of 2007 (H.R. 4106) was the subject of a hearing before the House Oversight and Government Reform Committee last spring. Both bills require that all Federal workers be considered eligible for telework unless the agency shows they are ineligible. Under current law, Federal workers must overcome the presumption that they are ineligible for telework unless the agency determines otherwise. However, while the bills require agencies to appoint a "telework managing officer" to report to Congress information on the number of workers involved in telework programs, they lack an enforcement mechanism if agencies fail to meet the telework requirement. The bills also do not address the right of unions to communicate or represent their members in telework situations, or address travel expense issues for workers who live outside the commuting area of their duty station but who are required to report to the office for meetings or other assignments, often at little notice and great expense to the worker.

While AFGE supports extending telework opportunities to all eligible employees, they also take the position that programs not interfere with the ability of unions to communicate with their members. Unions need to have access to the agency's e-mail system to broadcast information to the entire unit, including those who telework. In addition, union officials must be able to perform representation activities while teleworking. Further, like their office counterparts, teleworkers should still have full benefits of union membership. Workers who telecommute from outside the commuting area of their duty station should be compensated when they are required to travel to the office for meetings with their supervisors.

STEP ONE. OVERCOMING MANAGEMENT RESISTANCE

Remember

Telework yields multiple benefits to the Federal government, other public sector organizations, the private sector, the individual employee, and the community and has become increasingly prevalent in the modern workforce. Its results are so proven in fact, that Public Law 106-346 §359 requires Federal agencies to "establish a policy under which eligible employees of the agency may participate in telecommuting to the maximum extent possible without diminished employee performance."

The Arguments For Teleworking

Key benefits stemming from mainstream implementation of telework include:

- ☐ A workforce that teleworks on a regular basis is also capable of leveraging its decentralized work settings to maintain continuity of operations (COOP) in the face of a natural disaster, terrorist attack, or other emergency situation.
- ☐ Telework contributes to a greener environment by diminishing vehicle carbon emissions as a result of a truncated or nonexistent employee commute.
- ☐ The job performance of teleworkers has been documented to either exceed or remain on par with that of workers in a traditional workplace arrangement.
- ☐ Telework increases personal freedom and flexibility, thereby improving morale and decreasing stress.
- ☐ A strong telework program improves employee retention and recruitment by increasing an employer's attractiveness in the current competitive job market.
- ☐ Telework accommodates persons with disabilities.
- ☐ Telework permits more time for employees to care for their loved ones.
- ☐ Telework can enable reduced demand for office space as well as reduced facility operating costs.
- ☐ Telework allows for optimal use of technological advances.

Handbook for Managing Teleworkers – Toolkit

Continuity of Operations

Remember: Telework is a key factor in emergency planning, response, and prevention because it allows for the continuity of operations (COOP), or business continuity plans, where catastrophe would inhibit necessary protocol. Essentially, telework decentralizes and spreads the workforce to reduce the ratio of those impacted by a disaster. In fact, many public and private sector workplace policies now contain a telework component for COOP in the wake of the 2001 terrorist attacks, Hurricane Katrina, and potential pandemic or other widespread illnesses.

The George W. Bush administration, in particular, made clear the necessity for emergency planning and response. On May 3, 2006, President Bush issued the Implementation Plan for the National Strategy for Pandemic Influenza, which outlines the government's approach for dealing with the threat of pandemic influenza. It states: "All departments and agencies will be responsible for developing pandemic plans that … (2) ensure that the department or agency will be able to maintain its essential functions and services in the face of significant and sustained absenteeism."

To put absenteeism in a more quantitative sense, the Department of Health and Human Services expects a workplace absenteeism rate of up to 40 percent in the middle of a severe pandemic. The Telework Exchange reports that 73 percent of Federal employees assert that they will not show up at the office in the event of a pandemic outbreak and that only 27 percent of employees note that their agencies' COOP plans incorporate telework.

Remember: A telework program should not be merely delineated in a COOP plan, however. To be effective during an emergency, employees must already be actively teleworking, to smooth the transition from office to home and ensure security concerns are adequately addressed. This means as many employees as possible should already have telework capability including alternate site work arrangements, connectivity, necessary equipment, and frequent enough opportunities to telework so their systems have been tested and are functional.

The Scoop on COOP
What is a COOP plan?
A COOP plan is a plan developed for agencies to follow in the event of an incident situation (such as natural or human-made disaster) to maintain business operations. The plan should be sustainable for 30 days and include elements such as alternate facilities that could be operational within 12 hours of a disaster. The objective of COOP planning is to ensure the continuous performance of an agency's essential operations during an emergency; protect essential facilities, equipment, records, and other assets; reduce or mitigate disruptions to operations; reduce loss of life, minimize damage and losses; and achieve a timely and orderly recovery from an emergency and resumption of full service to customers.

What does a COOP plan entail?
Usually a COOP plan consists of plans and procedures, identification of essential elements, delegations of authority, orders of succession, alternate facilities, interoperable communications, vital records and databases, and tests, training, and exercises.

Step One. Overcoming Management Resistance

Where did COOP begin?

COOP essentially began in 1988, with the Executive Order 12656 that called for each agency to ensure it could continue to provide services during an emergency. Ten years later, the 1998 Presidential Decision Directive 67 stated that agencies should plan for all types of hazards, from floods and fires to terrorist attacks as well as alternate facilities that could be operational within 12 hours of a disaster and that the COOP operations should be sustainable for 30 days. In 2004, the Federal Preparedness Circular 65 was updated to establish standard elements for agencies' COOP plans and discusses how agencies can develop and implement their plans.

How are COOP and telework related?

Aside from telework's benefits such as employee work-life balance, increased productivity, and reduced operating costs, telework also enables continuous vital government services during a state of emergency. Continuity of operations relies more than ever on enabling government employees and contractors to work from any location. Therefore, a critical component of COOP planning is an information technology framework that enables secure, remote use of the same IT resources that would be accessed from the main office location. This infrastructure enables employees to work remotely at any time, not just in the event of a disaster.

Recent studies underscore the value of telework as a COOP measure. According to the Telework Exchange "COOP: A Wake Up Call" study, 40 percent of respondents believe their agency is not prepared to continue operating in the wake of a disaster. However, of respondents who indicated that their agency has a telework component in their COOP plans, 90 percent feel that their agency would be able to maintain business operations during a disaster. Additionally, according to a recent OPM study, 35 agencies have incorporated telework into their COOP programs, while another 37 say they are considering adding telecommuting to these initiatives.

Reduction of Energy Consumption and the Associated Carbon Footprint

Exorbitant gas prices; air pollution; irate, frustrated workers burning wasteful fuel sitting in traffic: America's post-industrial age has left modernized cities inundated with smog, vehicle emissions, and other environmental toxins. As we hand over our global home to posterity, we seek to buy less plastic, turn off the computer at night, use the recycling bin, and yes, even telework.

Remember

Telework curbs the emission of vehicle byproducts by keeping employees off the road or at least reducing their commute. As an added benefit, less time spent on the road also means less traffic congestion for those who choose to commute.

Domestically, the Federal government is seeking to preserve environmental purity, cut oil dependency, and help drivers save money. Telework researchers Kate Lister and Tom Harnish reviewed data from the Environmental Protection Agency (EPA), Department of Transportation (DOT), General Services Administration (GSA), and seven other sources and found that if 33 million Americans worked from home, Gulf oil imports could be reduced by 24-48 percent, greenhouse gases would be lowered by up to 67 million metric tons a year, and as much as 7.5 trillion gallons of gasoline each year would be saved, for a total of $110 million in savings a day. According to the Telework Exchange, if all eligible Federal employees teleworked two days per

Handbook for Managing Teleworkers – Toolkit

week, the Federal workforce would collectively save $3.3 billion and 2.7 million tons of pollutants annually.

Seeking to lead by example, the GSA determined the estimated savings based on a workforce of 12,205 teleworking one day per week. The environmental and other savings projections are based on fuel costs and other factors as of 9/3/07.

Total GSA Telework Work Trip Savings:

- 4,735,146 single occupancy vehicle miles.
- 220,239.3 gallons of gas.
- $615,789 fuel costs.
- 2,299.5 tons of emissions.

Remember: It is clear from the figures above that GSA telework alone can achieve significant reductions in vehicle emissions, refueling costs, and vehicle maintenance costs from extended wear and tear. And figures are expected to be even higher today since gas costs have increased dramatically since 2007.

Improved Performance

The current research consensus is that telework either improves job performance or maintains existing levels. According to a recent Telework Exchange study of Federal managers, 66 percent of managers who manage teleworkers find that teleworkers are as productive as their in-office counterparts. A considerable case in point is the U.S. Patent and Trademark Office's (PTO) telework program.

PTO has one of the largest telework programs in the Federal government because it established sound telework policies that led to maximum participation, abundant program support, and aggressive top level leadership. As of October 2007, there were 3,609 PTO employees participating in some form of telework. This represents an impressive 40.7 percent of PTO's total work force and 45.7 percent of total eligible employees.

PTO identified strong job performance as one of its key goals for its telework program. Examiners participating in one PTO pilot telework program showed a productivity increase of 10 percent with no difference in the quality of work. By 2003, there was so much interest in its telework pilot program that the agency needed to create a waiting list for participation. In part because of its use of telework, PTO has been recognized by Business Week magazine as one of the best places in America to launch a career and to round out one's career, and by Families magazine as one of the best places in the Washington area to work if you have a family.

Step One. Overcoming Management Resistance

While PTO may quantitatively assess productivity due to determining the amount of patents reviewed, many Federal agencies' productivity rates are not so easily calculated. There is no truly valid quantitative measure of typical white collar job performance. In spite of this however, even at jobs lacking the yardstick-type measurements used at PTO, there is ample evidence to suggest that telework has no impact on productivity and in some cases it is actually increased.

According to the Equal Employment Opportunity Commission's Office of the Inspector General, frequent teleworkers reported that they performed difficult work faster while at the home office (due to lack of frequent interruptions), lost no time due to traffic congestion or the stresses associated with commuting, and used less sick leave because healthcare providers were located closer to their homes.

A two-year study conducted on the productivity of a telework program at the Administrative Appeals Office in the Department of Justice (DOJ) on production-oriented tasks, i.e., adjudicative casework, showed an increase in productivity of approximately 71 percent. And at the National Energy and Water Management Center, telework afforded a 44 percent increase in productive person-hours.

There is a gamut of reasons telecommuting has the ability to increase productivity. Telecommuters typically find working at home to be more pleasant and less stressful, and people who enjoy their work and/or are less stressed are likely to be more productive. According to a study of the British communications agency, BT, "[m]ore than 90 percent of BT's teleworkers who responded to a European Union-backed survey said they experienced less stress and that their productivity increased." Also, certain tasks are easier to perform in specific environments. If a worker must read a mountain of reports, a quiet room at home is preferred to a busy office with distractions and frequent interruptions.

On the managerial side, telecommuting may improve performance by leading managers to measure performance primarily by results. Telecommuting pushes aside the justification of process and focuses on outcome. Essentially, managers and employees agree on which projects need to be completed and when, removing the need to constantly prove busyness at a desk.

Remember

This contrasts with the traditional office setting where there is more of a tendency for a manager to be impressed by those who spend long hours in the office. Such employees may indeed be hard-working, but staying behind a desk for a long period of time is not, in itself, evidence of high productivity. As a result then, the concept of work becomes more defined by accomplishing tasks, rather than maintaining a 9-to-5 schedule.

Another reason accounting for telework productivity may be that it allows workers the flexibility to schedule their work periods according to their natural productivity peaks thus

www.GovernmentTrainingInc.com

Handbook for Managing Teleworkers – Toolkit

optimizing output. If a manager tells a telecommuter to complete a report by 5 pm on Friday, the telecommuter can arrange his schedule any way he likes, as long as he meets his deadline.

Greater Flexibility, Morale, and Decreased Stress

Tips

Why crank on the engine and jump in the car to face a stressful commute when you can crank on the coffee maker and commute from your bedroom to another room in your home? Telework is becoming an increasingly popular alternative to driving the car or riding the train simply because it uses up less personal time, is more convenient, and cuts commuting costs.

Just how much free time is gained back? According to Telework Exchange, Americans spend more time commuting each year than on vacation, a shocking 245 hours on average. And teleworking just two days per week gets the typical Federal employee 98 hours of their life back. If time is money, then pocketing between 98-245 hours of time is cost worthy indeed! But the buck does not stop there.

Remember

Having more time to spend in a qualitative way rather than on a rush hour commute reduces stress and improves morale. One of the most consistent and common findings regarding telework benefits is reduced work-related stress. This reduction is due to decreased traffic headaches, a better work-life balance, more personal control over time and environment, and consequently, an increase in overall flexibility.

Telework also allows employees to be the determinants of their own schedule, so long as the number of hours worked or tasks completed is being met. For example, a teleworker beginning the workday at 8 am may opt to take a morning run at 10 am but replace the time by tacking on an extra half hour at the end of the day. In this way, teleworkers maintain productivity and feel less guilty about taking a break if they've run out of workflow inspiration; they may extend their work day and take a breather when they need it.

In addition to spending less on transportation costs and having fewer interruptions, telework allows for increased opportunity for appropriate meals and reduced exposure to contagious illness and/or unhealthy weather/air conditions.

For more information, a study by Ravi S. Gajendran and David A. Harrison of Pennsylvania State University summarizes multiple studies and provides empirical support for the work life benefits of telework.

Their conclusion: A common refrain in reviews of telecommuting research has been the inability, over 20 years of studies, to draw consistent conclusions about even its most basic consequences. Our results tackle some of these unknowns and suggest that telecommuting is likely more good than bad for individuals. Telecommuting has a clear upside: small but favorable effects on perceived autonomy, work– family conflict, job satisfaction, performance, turnover intent, and

Step One. Overcoming Management Resistance

stress. Contrary to expectations in both academic and practitioner literatures, telecommuting also has no straightforward, damaging effects on the quality of workplace relationships or perceived career prospects. However, there is a downside of higher intensity telecommuting in that it does seem to send coworker (but not supervisor) relationships in a harmful direction. Some of the complexities of these consequences have yet to be explored, but the evidence and theory reviewed here suggest that they can be managed effectively through informed human resources policies.[1]

Improved Recruitment, Retention, and Staffing

Despite the number of premature "retirement wave" predictions forecasting a major decrease in the government workforce, its inevitability is certain. The Office of Personnel Management anticipates that 40 percent of the Federal workforce will retire between 2006-15.

On the recruitment end of things, the incoming new generation of workers expects a more flexible work environment. This is the "digital" generation – one that has grown up in the era of computers and mobile technology. Telework Exchange's "Generation Y in the Federal IT Workplace" study notes that compressed workweek / telework options are key job perks.

"It feels normal for Gen Y employees to check in by BlackBerry all weekend as long as they have flexibility during the week. Sun Microsystem's telecommuting program, for example, has kicked into high gear in response to Generation Y's demands. Today more than half of Sun's employees work remotely."

Source: Telework Exchange. Generation Y in the Federal IT Workforce. Focus Group Report, November 2007.

Remember

On the retention end of things, the importance of retaining productive workers cannot be overstated, especially in a competitive job market. Along these lines, the Patent and Trademark Office (PTO) successfully implemented telework to counteract employee turnover and shortages. Largely as a result of the hoteling telework program it began in 2006, PTO has improved its ability to retain qualified workers and also expects to save on office space rental costs.

Additionally, effective succession planning requires that employers maintain occupational contact with retirees to facilitate a smooth and continuous transition of institutional knowledge and capability from one generation of workers to the next. Telework is a very appealing option for retirees willing to continue work with their former organizations.

Finally, telework increases flexibility on hiring and staffing options through the broadening the pool of exceptionally qualified people. This is due in part because telework allows an employer to hire employees living much further than within the driving/commuting distance of their place

---

1 The Good, the Bad, and the Unknown About Telecommuting: Meta-Analysis of Psychological Mediators and Individual Consequences. Ravi S. Gajendran and David A. Harrison. Journal of Applied Psychology. 2007. Vol. 92. No 6, 1524-1541.

Handbook for Managing Teleworkers – Toolkit

of employment. On the flip side, employers may also retain employees who want to relocate their residence beyond the local commuting area. This growing trend among employees is due to a variety of reasons such as maintaining family togetherness when a spouse wants/needs to relocate, the desire for a better quality of life provided by another location, the need to move for health-related reasons, etc.

Improved Accommodations for Persons with Disabilities

Remember

Telework improves accommodations for persons with disabilities who may prefer to work from the comfort of their home or are unable to work outside the home. While not all persons with disabilities need, or want, to work from home, telework is an option to those with reduced mobility and/or other impairment difficulties. The Bush Administration supported telework for these very benefits, stating in the President's New Freedom Initiative that the: *"Full inclusion of persons with disabilities into the workforce is an important goal not only because of the positive impact this will have on the worker, but also because of the benefits to the economy as a whole as production increases and people begin to leave government assistance....[of which may be realized by increasing] the number of employees with disabilities in the Federal workforce by implementing innovative hiring and working practices, including telework..."*

Jane Anderson, Executive Director for the Midwest Institute for Telecommuting Education, provided Congressional testimony on Telework for Persons with Disabilities. She stated that "The National Association for the Development of Disability Research in 1999 stated that the demand for telework from clients with multiple sclerosis continues to grow." Ms. Anderson provided multiple examples of telework benefitting those with disabilities and the employer – the persons with disabilities were able to work from home and the companies were not limited in their hiring. Additionally, many companies hired employees with disabilities to work off-peak hours. The persons would work evening or overnight shifts, allowing for 24-hour customer service.

Flexible Dependent Care

Remember

The personal freedom and flexibility of telework in turn allows for improved employee capability to care for loved ones. Essentially, those with children or ailing parents may use telework to increase their options for providing care while maintaining effective levels of work performance. This allows a person to be both employee and caretaker, removing the stress of leaving a dependent under the guidance of someone else, alone unattended, or with a caregiver who may only be present for a couple hours.

GSA published a report in August 2006 on dependent care and telework entitled "Is Standard Practice Best Practice? Emerging Perspective on Telework and Dependent Care." The report was based on research conducted by GSA focusing on employees teleworking from home. GSA surveyed 1,635 Federal teleworkers on their use of telework to assist with dependent care situations. 27 Federal agencies and sub-agencies participated in the survey. 53 percent of the respondents were taking care of dependents, and of those, 91 percent indicated that telework

Step One. Overcoming Management Resistance

aided them with their caretaking responsibilities. Furthermore, most of the 91 percent indicated that "telework benefited themselves as well as their dependents (happier, healthier) and their organizations (reduced turnover, improved job performance)."

Through telework, both the employer and the employee benefit from the reduced stress. Because telework allows such employees to perform their work and simultaneously have a comforting proximity to their dependents, they have lower stress levels and dependent care costs resulting in telework being a win-win situation for employer, caregiver, and dependent.

However, one of management's biggest concerns is that workers will be taking care of elders or children instead of doing their jobs. So specific arrangements should be spelled out before telework begins; avoiding untimely interruptions to workflow, with clear arrangements made as to specific care. For example, a babysitter may be on site while the worker is at home; or an elder might be at a senior center during working hours.

Must Do

Office Space and Operating Cost Savings

Another benefit of telework is that it can result in reduced demand and associated costs for office space, technology costs, and costs in other organization operations. Successful telework programs characterized by aggressive top level support, solid program design, and clear measures, such as those at GSA, Treasury Inspector General for Tax Administration, and PTO (U.S. Patent and Trademark Office), all reported significant space savings.

Remember

GSA published a report in 2006 based on an assessment of 20 Federal agencies' current telework programs. Using estimated averages based on agency survey responses, the report determined that an investment of approximately $16 million over three years towards a "basic" teleworker-at-home solution for 50,000 teleworkers at an agency with a total staff of 100,000 can, in appropriate circumstances, be offset with a realization of over $36 million in benefits over the same three-year period. These benefits were noted to have come through cost savings achieved from human resource improvements (such as reduced employee absences), reduced real estate demands, reduced employee retention costs, and improved productivity savings.

For a "do-it-yourself" method, GSA developed a tool called the "Cost Per Person Model" (CPPM) that enables agencies to assess the "break-even" point between the cost of additional telework (IT and connectivity) and the savings from reduced real estate use. A copy of the CPPM may be requested online at http://www.gsa.gov/cppm. For documented space savings, visit http://www.gsa.gov/telework. Information can be found under Where to Work>Alternative Officing>Library> Case Studies. You can also go to Basics >Guidance and Studies >Telework Technology Cost Study.

Optimal Use of Technological Advances

Remember Understated but nevertheless important is the potential of telework to facilitate the optimal use of existing and cutting edge workplace technology. This is an ironic twist since it is widely held that technology enables telework. However, telework is responsible for enabling the use of technology because most advances in workplace technology are highly suited for mobility and telecommunications required by telework – products that are lighter, more portable, more virtual, more responsive, and so on.

The benefit of promoting the use of current technology is twofold, as the use of such requires on-the-job training to familiarize employees with electronic equipment. This naturally keeps the workforce adept and sharp in the use of workplace technology.

The optimal use of technology ultimately increases return on technology investments, increases employee productivity through streamlined asset functionality, increases workforce mobility and flexibility, improves capability in emergency (COOP) situations, and maintains an up-to-date technologically-capable workforce.

Issues For Managers

Remember Faced with managing teleworkers for the first time, many managers have reservations. Managing "people you can't see" can be very different to the way employees are normally managed. There are five common issues that need to be considered

- ☐ Control
- ☐ Trust
- ☐ Performance management
- ☐ Communication
- ☐ Telework is "different"

Control

Although telework initiatives help to create a flexible workplace, this has little to do with managers losing control. Well-designed telework arrangements provide tools that managers can use to retain the level of control they need.

Remember Telework is a voluntary, cooperative arrangement between an employee and a manager: managers shouldn't feel forced to allow an employee to telework. Assessment questionnaires and formal discussions are normally required before an employee can qualify for telework, allowing for control, even before the employee begins his or her responsibilities.

Although managers should not normally withhold approval for qualifying staff, there are some reasons that telework could be denied. These relate to job requirements, past and present levels of performance and other work related issues.

Step One. Overcoming Management Resistance

Once telework has been approved, managers can supervise the arrangement. They can also influence:

- ☐ The length of any initial trial period. This could be used if there is serious doubt about whether the arrangement will work.
- ☐ The hours and days that telework can take place and when meetings will require attendance at the office.
- ☐ Appropriate performance requirements and task lists although the same standards should also apply to non-teleworking staff.

Teleworking staff are not normally out of the office full time, but even if the program does evolve into full-time telework, at that point the manager is usually experienced and confident enough to deal with employees remotely, regardless of hours worked.

One of the major benefits of telework is that employees have better control of their own work outcomes. With appropriate performance management managers can develop enhanced control of the projects and initiatives.

> In many telework initiatives, managers find they have more direct control than in the traditional environment. Such managers have thought about various issues involved and taken appropriate action.
>
> *Remember*

Trust

The development of trust is discussed extensively in Step Four. Some studies of trust and mistrust have concluded that it is a major problem for telework managers of teleworkers, while others found that managers have few if any trust-related problems. A 2004 Toshiba study found that mistrust was the third most important problem, coming after supervision challenges and concern about lower work motivation but before technology, communication and productivity issues.[2]

Performance Management

Managing performance is a fairly simple process—define the job, communicate requirements, monitor that requirements are being met, and recognize and reward progress. These basic elements should be the same, regardless of whether the employee is teleworking.

The job definition should also be identical—it'll be just as important, have the same components, and the same measurements should apply to component tasks. The only variation would be where the components of the job can best be performed. Discussing this could help the teleworker plan his or her days both at and away from the office.

---

[2] Mobility and Mistrust, an independent study commissioned by Toshiba Australia, September 2204

Tips: When it comes to communicating job requirements, the job description should be identical for both teleworkers and other staff. However, you might want to provide more detailed process guides (if applicable) than would be necessary for nonteleworkers. Discussions and briefings can be scheduled for when the teleworker is in the office and the telephone and email can easily substitute when necessary.

Action plans and 'to do' lists can be a useful communication tool when managing teleworkers. They provide an ongoing reminder of priority tasks and help maintain focus and productivity. They can also help monitor performance and provide an 'agenda' for any conversations with managers and colleagues when they are back in the office.

Key performance indicators and project milestones should also be the same for teleworkers and office workers. Taking the effort to meet and discuss team performance and its contribution to the organization's goals could be more important for the teleworker than it is for other staff as it keeps them in touch with what is happening around the organization. An individual teleworker's performance should also be discussed on a regular basis.

Tips: The answer to the question "How do I manage staff I can't see?" is usually another question: "How do you manage staff now?" If managers already manage on the basis of resourcing and measuring outcomes, very little change will be required when an employee becomes a teleworker.

Communication

Tips: Many managers are concerned about how they will stay in touch once several staff members are working offsite. There are a number of ways to effectively communicate with teleworkers, including phone, email, via a secure site on the Internet, and the office Intranet, in addition to scheduled team and project meetings as well as social gatherings and one-to-one meetings.

The teleworker can plan "office" days around scheduled meetings and supervisors and others can plan meetings for days when the teleworker in the office. This is even easier if teleworkers are only out of the office a few days a week. Unscheduled one-to-one meetings in person, could be difficult for the teleworker although many such meetings can easily and more efficiently be handled over the phone or by email.

Access to informal and after hours social gatherings could be difficult for teleworkers, and unfortunately there is no easy answer to this. For a few days a week, the teleworker will be away from these social loops. However, many teleworkers choose this option so they work without interruption, and don't mind missing out on gossip and unscheduled or unimportant meetings. Furthermore, email and phone can easily be used to arrange informal social gatherings such as lunch, or a drink after work.

Step One. Overcoming Management Resistance

> Most teleworkers are not disadvantaged by being out of the office for a couple of days a week, particularly if managers and colleagues schedule important meetings for the days the teleworker is physically present. *— Remember*

Communicating Effectively

> You can make communication more effective and efficient in several ways. Notice boards should be centrally located both electronically (on the Intranet) and in the office and should be used for all announcements and news. All staff should be allowed to post notices. This ensures that employees know where to look for news, that they check back often, and that they feel involved. *— Tips*

Create a meeting calendar of all scheduled meetings on the Intranet. Agendas should also be published. All meetings should be scheduled and posted with as much lead time as possible.

The Intranet can also include a staff directory with links to individual profiles. Such facilities can support social interaction even among physically remote workers. All staff should be familiar with address lists and the 'reply to all' function built into most email software. Remember, however, that the 'reply to all' function should only be used for work-related items.

The use of 'real-time' messaging and chat options should be explored so all employees, regardless of location, can quickly contact each other. Many of these services include a 'presence indicator' so everyone knows who else is online at any given time. Consideration should be given to the use of online meeting options. These range from circulating a document for comments to more comprehensive meeting tools.

Teleconferencing should be investigated. This includes both audio and videoconferencing. (Meeting processes might need some changes to ensure that everyone can contribute.)

All meetings, whether electronic or in person, should include an update on upcoming events and meetings.

Minutes of all meetings should be archived where attendees can easily refer to them, whether they are offsite or not.

> All employees should be encouraged to include alternative contact numbers and/or email addresses on their voicemail. This can ensure that individuals will always be able to contact each other, regardless of location. *— Tips*

Telework agreements should state when staff will be available and should include teleworkers work hours as well as the core times when they will be available. All relevant colleagues and managers should be aware of and respect these times.

Tips: Managers should make an effort to check in with their teleworkers when they return to the office—to see if everything's OK, remind them of any important events, and reestablish contact. Although most teleworkers are fairly good at staying in touch with the office, even when they're offsite, a quick chat with the manager is usually valuable.

Finally, it is a good idea to start your telework initiative with a launch function. This informal celebration will help create a successful team.

Telework Is "Different"

Perhaps the greatest challenge that new managers of telework face is the perception that it is 'different'. But is it really that different from the way things are happening now?

Telework means that employees are not at their desk or even in the office all the time but that's not unusual. Many employees are away from their desks in the course of a normal working week. There are meetings in the office and offsite, people pop out for lunch and other quick shopping trips and some staff will spend a lot of time liaising with other workers away from their desk. Furthermore, some employees already take work home, working at weekends to meet deadlines, during illness, or covering important domestic issues. Many could also be checking their emails from home after hours.

Telework changes the location at which work is performed but not the job, performance monitors don't change, and meetings can still be scheduled. The work still happens.

Even if telework does seem to be very different, such alternative working arrangements are often considered by organizations as part of planning for business continuity threats such as terrorism, natural disasters or pandemics. Managers who accept that working off site is a normal and acceptable option will be in a much better position to handle such events if they happen.

Q & A: What About Me – The Manager?

A successful telework program can improve organizational efficiency, raise the quality and quantity of work, boost employee morale and job satisfaction, and lower your employee turnover rate. In addition, the enhanced communication that a telework program fosters can further develop your own skills as a manager.

How productive are employees when they are not in the office?

Tips: Many teleworkers report that they are able to focus on work better without the distractions of the office. The Maryland Department of Transportation reported a 27 percent increase in productivity due to telework, and American Express employees who telework produce 43 percent more business than their non-teleworking counterparts. In addition, managers are usually pleasantly surprised to find that their employees are more accessible while teleworking.

Step One. Overcoming Management Resistance

How do you know that teleworkers are working?

From their results--if a teleworker is not finishing assignments or meeting deadlines, you'll know. Set objectives, trust that your teleworkers are spending their time wisely, and then review how each one is able to meet his or her goals. Most importantly, pick the right people for the program. If an employee performs well in the office, most likely they'll perform well away from the office.

Remember

Will I ever see the teleworker?

The manager decides when and how often a teleworker is away from the office. Most teleworkers aren't away from the office more than one or two days a week. And again, communication doesn't stop when the employee is teleworking. Instead, some of the face-to-face communication is replaced with the phone, email, videoconferencing, and instant messaging.

How difficult and costly is it to establish and administer the program?

This depends on several factors:

☐ Size of agency and number of teleworkers
☐ Type of information technology used
☐ Goals of program

The process for setting up a telework program can be as simple as:

☐ Developing a written policy and employee agreement
☐ Announcing the program to staff
☐ Selecting and training participants
☐ Providing necessary equipment and secure remote access capabilities

Implementing the program

Organizations often start with a small-scale pilot program, which they later expand after gaining experience through the pilot. It's also helpful to have a designated telework "champion" to oversee the process and work with other key individuals within the organization, such as information technology personnel, human resources personnel, and the facilities management staff.

For more information see Handbook for Managing Teleworkers, published by Government Training Inc. (www.governmenttraininginc.com/index.asp#Bookstore)

Large-scale programs include a major commitment to planning and implementing. The involvement of the IT Department is extremely important. A telework program sometimes requires continued investments of money and staff, but these costs are quickly recovered in other savings (i.e., real estate, parking, improved efficiency, reduced retention/recruitment costs). In some cases, the return on investment (ROI) can be as high as 200 percent to 1,500 percent after three years.

How does working at home affect dependent care issues?

Must Do: Teleworkers should understand that teleworking is not a substitute for dependent care. Although teleworking may be attractive to people who want to be closer to home for personal reasons, dependent care arrangements still need to be made. This principle should be included in your program's telework agreement, which all teleworkers sign.

Who pays for charges such as increased electricity and phone charges?

Many employers pay for agency phone calls, but not for increased electricity from computer use. This should also be noted in the telework agreement.

Is there an ideal percentage of employees who should telework?

This depends on the nature of your business, the type of work performed by employees, the suitability of an employee to work away from the office, the corporate culture, the technology available, and the interest of employees.

Will everyone want to telework?

Tips: Most likely not all of your employees will want to telework. Local studies have shown that approximately 23 percent of office workers "could and would" telework if given the opportunity to do so. Some employees prefer to keep their home and workplace separate, others prefer the social contact with work colleagues, and some may have jobs unsuitable for teleworking. Managers can offer a range of options for teleworking, from just one day per month to only in special situations such as inclement weather to several or more days per week. Keeping an open mind and selecting the right candidates for your program will ensure success.

How does teleworking affect morale and productivity among workers who continue to work onsite?

When a telework program is implemented properly and the teleworker selection process is clear and objective, negative effects on the morale and productivity of office workers can be minimized. Clearly communicate to all employees that teleworkers are selected on the basis of their job functions and their work performance characteristics. An employee's telework arrangement should also not increase the other employees' workloads. When management fails to handle the transition carefully, objectively and transparently, jealousy and resentment can arise from nonteleworkers who mistakenly believe that teleworkers are not really working. If the situation is properly handled among coworkers uninterested in teleworking, they will likely respect those who do.

Step One. Overcoming Management Resistance

Managers need to ensure that all employees are treated equitably when it comes to expectations and performance, regardless of where they are working. Employees who telework more than two or three days per week should be encouraged to visit the office to maintain personal relationships with colleagues and supervisors. As with any organizational change or shift, communication is the key to its success!

Must Do

Will teleworking cause extra work for other colleagues? Will they be burdened with teleworkers' work?

This is a common myth, but implemented properly, a telework program should not cause any extra work for nonteleworkers.

Do I need to have a pilot program?

A pilot program can offer your agency a test run on teleworking without full immersion. It's a great way to experiment with how a telework program will affect your agency, helping you find out what works and what doesn't, and allowing you to improve shortcomings before a full-fledged execution. Pilot programs should have a cross-section of positions, staff, and systems.

Tips

Will employees and supervisors need training before beginning a teleworking arrangement?

Introducing a telework program can be a major change in the way an organization does business; hence, training is strongly recommended. Telework!VA provides both onsite and online training for teleworkers, nonteleworkers, and managers. At a minimum, training should cover your organization's telework policy and agreement, eligibility criteria based on the job and employee characteristics, establishing trust, improving communication, planning and organization, home office set-up, remote access procedures, IT security and performance.

Must Do

How do I ensure safety and ergonomic issues?

It is the employee's responsibility to maintain a safe and productive home office environment. This is typically addressed in the telework policy, by having the employee complete a home office safety checklist and through training. There are a variety of online resources that can assist the teleworker in ensuring that their alternate work site is safe, and help them understand how ergonomics can affect their physical well-being.

Can I require employees to telework?

Private sector employers can require teleworking as part of their working arrangement, but most experts do not recommend this unless the employee was hired under a telework/remote work provision. Forcing an employee to telework may be counterproductive, and while a job may be suitable for teleworking, some employees' personalities are not. Some people feel out of the loop and isolated working offsite. Others have difficulty managing their time independently, or are not able to block out distractions in a remote office environment.

No No

www.GovernmentTrainingInc.com

What if teleworking doesn't work?

Tips

Sometimes this does occur. If a teleworker's quality of work declines, treat it as you would any performance issue. Review the telework agreement and give your employees a chance to improve. Your telework agreement should include a clause stating that either the employer or the employee can cancel the telework agreement for operational or performance issues. If projects or environments change, then the teleworking program might have to change too.

Are there any union issues concerning teleworking?

By their nature, unions are designed to look after their members' best interests, and thus, frequently are very interested in the issues surrounding telework. Some of the concerns that unions have raised over the years involve ensuring an equitable selection process, allowing employees in the policy development process, and avoiding higher production goals that are not accompanied by a commensurate increase in compensation. Companies with unions should approach and work with them from the onset of the program.

So, will telework work for me?

Telework requires careful management if it is going to be effective but the reservations commonly associated with issues such as control, trust, performance management, and communication are, arguably, unfounded. Consider the following:

- ☐ Managers rarely lose control of their teleworkers. In fact, well set up telework initiatives can provide managers with more control.
- ☐ Most managers already trust their employees to perform the work expected of them and work towards increasing that trust.
- ☐ Most aspects of performance management can remain the same once telework has started.
- ☐ Most existing communication modes remain effective once telework starts and, with only a few alterations, staying in touch in a "distributed" environment becomes easier.
- ☐ Working away from the traditional office is already an accepted option for many people.

Tips

Effective management of a work force that includes teleworkers generally relies on three things. The first is to choose appropriate tasks and individuals. The second is to recognize that the only thing that should change once a telework arrangement has been set up is the location where the work is performed. The third is that the telework arrangement should be accepted as part of the "corporate culture."

After realizing that the only thing that's changing is the work location, answering other questions becomes easier:

- ☐ Turn the question around, what will be changing for office workers?

Step One. Overcoming Management Resistance

☐ What is the present process?

☐ Will the present process work when the work location changes?

If the answer is 'Yes', the present process can continue without alteration. If the answer is 'No', ask what difference the work location has made. How should the process be amended?

Make the required amendment and ensure that it applies to both teleworkers and nonteleworkers alike. Utilizing the same management process for both teleworkers and office workers is an important part of making the telework arrangement 'normal', i.e. an accepted work option. It helps reduce favoritism and confusion, helps teleworkers feel part of the organization, and helps realize the full benefits of telework. Only when the culture of the organization shifts to being 'location-independent' will management challenges reduce and the full benefits of telework become accessible.

Myths and Misperceptions

Even after considering all the previously addressed issues, questions and misperceptions about telecommuting may linger. The following are some of the most commonly shared myths about telecommuting.

MYTH # 1 There is no way to judge whether telecommuters are really working. They could be taking the day off.

The employee's completed work products or progress reports will show whether work is being accomplished. Managers of telecommuters should focus on the quality, quantity, and timeliness of work products. Managers should manage by results, rather than by observation. For those whose results are difficult to define using traditional performance measurements, performance expectations may be developed and refined through systematic progress reporting by the telecommuter. The manager and the employee should establish goals and objectives together.

MYTH # 2 Employees work less if left unsupervised.

Survey results show marked improvements in productivity, often because employees have fewer distractions and interruptions and are less stressed due to the absence of a commute to work. Employees who have demonstrated their commitment to work at the traditional office typically exhibit the same or a greater level of commitment at the alternate work site. In fact, as opposed to working less, the reported tendency is for telecommuters to work much more, sometimes to the point of excess.

MYTH # 3 Social interaction cannot be maintained between telecommuters and their colleagues.

There are many techniques for overcoming feelings of isolation, including telecommuting for only a portion of the workweek, core days in the office, and regular communication by telephone, voice mail or other communications media. Telecommuters should be included in all scheduled meetings and events and should receive all office correspondence.

MYTH # 4 I won't be able to reach my employees when I need them. What if a crisis comes up?

Managers can set the hours that employees are available by telephone or require telecommuters to call in at specified times. Also ask yourself: When a crisis happens now, is everyone available? Some people are out sick, some are on travel, and others are offsite in meetings. With a successful telecommuting program, managers know where employees are and can usually reach them by telephone. Many managers say the planning that goes into telecommuting eliminates some of the crisis management entirely.

MYTH # 5 Our office requires a relatively formal structure. Telecommuting is too unstructured for such an environment.

Telecommuting is flexible, but that does not equate to unstructured. Managers often use a telecommuter agreement to spell out what is expected of an employee, and supervisors and telecommuters agree on tasks and due dates.

MYTH # 6 Telecommuting is a nice, simple solution for any issues my organization faces.

Any successful telecommuting program recognizes that telecommuting is just one tool to help solve the complex problems facing today's government organizations. It is hardly a panacea for social difficulties or dumping ground for nonperformers.

MYTH # 7 Supervisors should feel grateful to be able to participate in a telecommuting program.

Supervisors and managers often view telecommuting as a favor that can do for their employees, without any consideration for the tremendous benefits they gain from a telecommuting arrangement. In terms of productivity, flexible work arrangements allow participants and their organizations to take greater advantage of peaks in employee productivity. In fact, rather than being seen as a benefit or a reward, telework should be viewed as a viable human resources and work option. Making it appear as a benefit or reward might create unnecessary resentment in the office.

Overcoming Management Resentment

A July 2010 survey by the nonprofit Partnership for Public Service and management consultants Booz Allen Hamilton found that management resistance is still a major obstacles to telework. Their Executive Summary states:

"One can only imagine the disruption to vital Federal government services if terrorists detonated a 'dirty' bomb in Washington, D.C., and brought the nation's capital to a standstill, or if an influenza pandemic spread across the country and indefinitely kept tens of thousands of civil servants quarantined and away from their offices.

The Federal government's ability to protect the nation's security and meet essential public needs would be undermined if these or a wide range of other unexpected and uncontrollable events kept employees off the job for long periods of time—making it imperative that the government be prepared to continue effective operations under all circumstances.

Such preparation must include a robust policy that builds teleworking—the ability to work from home or from a remote location—into the fabric of the civil service as one means of helping ensure the continuity of government operations during times of crisis."

Step One. Overcoming Management Resistance

Remember: This may seem simple enough. Rapid advances in technology have made working from a remote location much easier and more efficient than ever before, and there has been a growing consensus that telework has a number of significant economic benefits for the government and work-life advantages for its employees.

Yet to date, all of the talk about the desirability of telework in government has led to insufficient progress and action.

The Partnership for Public Service and Booz Allen Hamilton examined the current state of teleworking and four other flexible work arrangements—compressed workweeks, flextime, part-time schedules and job sharing—to better understand their use in the Federal government today, to identify the impediments being encountered and to determine what approaches will be most effective to removing barriers.

They reported, "We have concluded that if all the talk about telework is to be translated into concrete action, the government must take a different approach—an approach that will change the current mindset of managers, set aggressive goals, start with the premise of "yes" and ensure that teleworking can be effective during a crisis."

The Federal government must begin operating on the assumption that all employees are eligible to telework unless managers can demonstrate why it is not appropriate, a shift from the current practice that tends to put the onus on the workers and accepts inconsistent standards across the government.

The government also must set aggressive targets for teleworking and not be satisfied with small incremental advances. The Obama administration has set a goal of having 150,000 employees teleworking by 2011, a positive first step. We propose a goal of 600,000 Federal civil servants teleworking by 2014.

Must Do: To meet aggressive targets, government managers must embrace a different outlook. Currently, managers tend to view telework as an employee perk, rather than a smart business practice that can save money on overhead, provide better citizen services by extending hours and ensure continuity of operations during regional or national emergencies. They also tend to wrongly assume physical presence equals strong performance, often because better performance measures are not available to them.

Moreover, the ability to work remotely must be viewed as a national security imperative, and that capacity should be tested regularly so that agencies can analyze their capabilities, shore up weaknesses and ensure telework is fully incorporated in all agency continuity of operations plans.

Overall, the Federal government, once a leader in teleworking and other work flexibilities, has clearly lost its momentum and, to its detriment, is significantly underutilizing some of these important tools.

www.GovernmentTrainingInc.com

Here are the facts.

- According to the government's own data, less than 6 percent of all full-time Federal workers telework even one day a month—just 102,900 Federal employees of the 1.9 million on the government payroll when the Federal survey was conducted in 2008.
- Agencies inconsistently implement telework programs, with wide discrepancies in use, approaches and technologies across the Federal government.
- Although the number of teleworkers increased slightly in 2008, annual government surveys show a consistent drop in teleworking from 2004 through 2007. The number peaked at 140,694 in 2004 but plummeted to 94,643 in 2007.
- Job sharing and part-time schedules are rarely used in the Federal government. As of September 2009, 3.3 percent of Federal employees worked part-time and .02 percent job shared. Comparable data currently do not exist for compressed workweeks and flex schedules, although to the government's credit, agency work-life coordinators assert that participation rates in these programs are high and have been successfully embedded in the Federal work-life culture.
- Only 44 of 78 agencies, or 56 percent of Federal organizations, have integrated telework into their formal continuity of operations planning—a crucial element needed to make sure essential employees can support agency missions and meet important public needs during a natural disaster or a crisis such as a terrorist attack or a pandemic.
- Due to the underutilization of telework, part-time work and job sharing, the majority of Federal agencies are missing out on the opportunity to reap savings on real estate, infrastructure, basic operating costs and energy usage, and to improve their business processes and increase productivity. The Patent and Trademark Office has proven this can be done, savings millions of dollars on office expenses and creating the capability to add more than 1,000 examiners a year without adding extra real estate or parking facilities.
- Few Federal agencies make use of flexible work arrangements as a strategic tool to recruit and retain top talent, or to broadly help employees balance family and work obligations, and reduce lengthy commuting times and transportation costs.

Our study found that a number of factors are impeding the use and growth of teleworking in the Federal government, including management resistance, cultural and organizational barriers, and technology and information security concerns.

A survey released by the Office of Personnel Management (OPM) in 2009 revealed that about half of the Federal agencies cited management resistance as a barrier to the use of telework, a theme that was prevalent in our extensive discussions with work-life coordinators, teleworkers, thought leaders, union officials and senior executives.

Step One. Overcoming Management Resistance

As a general proposition, government managers were concerned about limited productivity and inaccessibility of teleworkers; the potential for abuse; a lack of accountability; and the absence of personal interaction.

In addition, our study found that some managers were simply unaware of workplace flexibilities, including the job sharing option.

We also found that some employees were uneasy about the lack of face-to-face contact with their managers when teleworking. Furthermore, in most agencies, eligibility for telework is determined either by position or by individual, creating confusion and even resentment when some employees see their colleagues teleworking while they are not eligible themselves.

Another barrier centered on technology, with agency officials citing concerns about teleworkers using unsecured networks and access to classified information in non-secure locations. An additional technological barrier to telework has been the lack of a clear policy about who provides equipment and services.

Agencies can and have overcome these roadblocks. Organizations such as the Patent and Trademark Office (PTO), the Defense Information Systems Agency (DISA) and the Nuclear Regulatory Commission (NRC) have set an example by implementing pilot programs, addressing security barriers and expanding telework to improve the way they conduct business and serve the public.

Both Congress and the Obama administration have recognized the benefits of workplace flexibilities and currently are taking steps to increase the use of teleworking. Legislation in the House and Senate, for example, would make substantive changes in telework eligibility, use, training and continuity planning. The administration, meanwhile, has a short-term plan to increase the number of teleworkers, and OPM has begun a pilot project with its own workforce that is allowing 400 staff members to individually determine where and when work will be accomplished.

While these are important efforts, much more can and should be done. Based on our review of the literature, extensive interviews, focus groups and analysis of survey data, we recommend that:

- ☐ The Federal government should significantly increase the use of teleworking, setting an ambitious goal for half of the nearly 1.2 million eligible Federal employees, or about 600,000 civil servants, to be engaged in telework by 2014 in order to match the private-sector companies with strong and effective telework programs. To achieve this goal, government- wide guidance is needed. All employees should be eligible to telework unless a supervisor or manager can demonstrate why an employee is not eligible. Each agency with fewer than 50 percent of its eligible employees teleworking should develop an action plan with annual updates to achieve the goal.

Handbook for Managing Teleworkers – Toolkit

- ☐ OPM should determine an appropriate goal to spur an increase in the number of part-time and job sharing opportunities and encourage agencies to inform employees these options are available.

- ☐ Congress should approve legislation to increase the strategic use of telework in Federal agencies, create a framework to boost the number of employees eligible to telework, and place responsibility in the hands of senior leaders for coordinating telework activity. The key elements in any final bill should include telework's role in agency mission continuity plans, collaboration between agencies, the role of the telework managing officer and clear reporting requirements, telework definitions and participation guidelines.

! Must Do Agencies must link telework to mission continuity plans. Unexpected events and emergencies have proven that telework can be an effective way for agencies to continue to operate during a crisis, and all agencies, regardless of whether Congress approves pending telework legislation, should incorporate telework into their continuity plans.

- ☐ The General Services Administration (GSA), as part of its facility and long range master planning services for Federal agencies, should advise agencies on how to reduce their real estate footprint through telework. The Office of Management and Budget (OMB) should require that an agency's use of teleworking and remote offices be reflected in all construction project or facility expansion budgets, and should require agencies to strategically assess how remote office use can reduce the need for permanent space.

! Must Do Agencies must solve the information security challenges, including developing secure telework architecture and authentication solutions, and addressing other technical issues related to employees working from remote locations. The Federal Chief Information Officer (CIO), located in OMB, is ideally positioned to bring together top agency officials and thought leaders on information security.

- ☐ Senior leaders must set the tone within their agencies and ensure that those participating in flexible work arrangements are held to the same performance standards—no more and no less—as their colleagues who do not participate in such programs.

- ☐ OPM should monitor and evaluate agency flexible work arrangement programs to obtain a complete picture of how these approaches are being used across the entire government. In addition, key metrics should be used to assess and improve individual flexible work arrangement programs at the agency level by documenting the impact and benefits, and identifying issues that need correction.

Step One. Overcoming Management Resistance

Case Study: Working Together: Teleworkers and Managers
On June 10, 2009, Virginia Governor Timothy Kaine issued an Executive Order to "green" Virginia –calling for a statewide Telework Day. The Commonwealth of Virginia, Telework!VA, and Telework Exchange encouraged organizations and individuals to telework from home or a remote location on Monday August 3 –Telework Day.

The following illustrates the impact of a single day, captures feedback from participants, and demonstrates the potential for telework to deliver significant time, environmental, and cost savings.

- Telework Day Snapshot: 4,267 employees teleworked on Telework Day –22 percent of participants never teleworked before Telework Day; 95 percent of participants located in Virginia
- A Day Can Make a Difference: Telework Day participants realized significant savings–approximately $124,000 across the United States, and $113,000 in Virginia
- Want a Raise?: Teleworking one day per week delivers approximately $2,000 in savings to each teleworker annually
- Be the Change: As Telework Day demonstrated, teleworkers take cars off the road, save energy, and remove pollutants from the air. In one day, participants:
- Avoided driving more than 155,782 miles
- Removed 82.77 tons of pollutants from the air
- Productivity Impact: 69 percent of Virginia Telework Day participants said they accomplished more than on a typical day at the office
- Looking Forward: 91 percent of Virginia Telework Day participants say they are now more likely to telework in the future

Lessons Learned – Teleworkers Talk
What surprised you about teleworking on Telework Day?
"I knew that I could work at home, but I didn't realize that my home office environment would increase my productivity significantly."

"How apparently unprepared the …wide area network was for handling mass remote access. I normally work at home four days per week under ADA –telecommuting day was really, really slow."

"I forwarded my office phone and answered e-mails promptly –surprising people at how quickly things were done. And yet I also got e-mails that said, "Oh, you aren't in today, I'll talk to you tomorrow." I then called people to remind them that telework means teleWORK!"

What is the most important part of successful teleworking ?
"The leadership in the agency/business must fully support and encourage it."

"Ability to connect to everything you normally would be able to if sitting at your desk."

"Planning my work around teleworking, because there are some work tasks that I cannot do from home (for example, direct consumer services). I make sure that those types of tasks are covered, then schedule a 'paperwork' day at home for case management activities."

"Connectivity to coworkers/clients."

"Most important is having an environment conducive to working; i.e. quiet surroundings, ability to connect to your network, etc."

Handbook for Managing Teleworkers – Toolkit

🚩 The Big Picture: Tips On Telework Programs

Remember

- ☐ Stay informed about the provisions of the telework programs to assist your employees as they submit requests or make inquiries.

- ☐ Remind employees on a regular basis that the telework program exists to help them meet personal challenges and expand professional opportunities.

- ☐ Be sure to consider the needs of all your employees, those who apply for participation in telework programs and those that do not choose to participate in telework programs but whose work may be affected by the proposed arrangement.

- ☐ Create an environment that fosters employee initiative and creativity. Engage your employees—those participating in a telework program and others who might be affected by it—in efforts to develop effective working relationships. This includes effective communication between staff members over time.

- ☐ Be ready to work with employees who encounter difficulties making a new working arrangement successful. Remind them that different work styles and approaches can yield valuable results.

- ☐ Keep the different telework programs in mind as you engage in workload planning for your office. Such efforts may yield valuable insights for your employees as they request to work in a nontraditional work situation.

- ☐ Ensure the confidentiality of employees who apply for telework programs.

- ☐ Review employee applications for the telework program to make sure they are completed correctly. Identify and resolve issues early. As appropriate, follow up on the approval process to ensure a decision is made in a timely manner.

- ☐ Be fair in your consideration of applications for the telework program. Treat employees equitably. Be prepared to give sound business reasons for your decisions to accept or deny an application.

- ☐ Be prepared to clearly communicate why some occupations allow for nontraditional work situations while others do not. When managers do not clearly articulate the parameters for participation in the program, assumptions by all parties are made that can lead to misconceptions, gossip, internal office conflict, or formal grievances.

- ☐ Share "lessons learned," "best practices," and "problems to avoid" with other supervisors and managers.

Ensure Employee Success

🚩 *Remember*
Be clear about expected levels of performance. Make sure your employees understand their job responsibilities thoroughly. As appropriate, before authorizing participation in the various telework programs, provide training, mentoring, and/or job shadowing on skills an employee needs in a nontraditional work situation—or to prepare to function in one. Training might include courses in communication, time management, teamwork, and customer service.

Support employee efforts to be accountable and work independently. When appropriate, consider having your employee prepare status reports on a regular basis that indicate job responsibilities and deadlines, changes, issues, and proposed remedies. Encourage employee initiative. Help employees develop their skills at managing themselves and their projects.

Step One. Overcoming Management Resistance

Promote your employees' empowerment. Look for ways to capitalize on their creativity and enthusiasm.

Consider how employee performance and morale may improve from a work situation that better reflects their personal needs and/or professional interests, yet meets the needs of the organization.

Promote techniques that foster good relationships with peers and customers. Take steps to ensure effective collaboration, especially between the employees that are operating in a nontraditional work situation and those who work in the office every day. Provide onsite staff with contact information for teleworkers, and encourage them to call if they have questions or need information. Have employees in a nontraditional work situation explain how they will keep involved and up to date with team projects.

Provide training to all members of the office to help them perform "backup" roles and providing mentoring, job shadowing, and/or cross-training to back-ups.

Support employees who want to work in nontraditional work situations but who might not be fully qualified. Help employees identify their learning objectives for a task or the professional capability they are trying to acquire. Work with them to determine the support they need (e.g., more guidance from you on how to perform the skill, more frequent feedback during critical learning phases, formal training).

Address Job Requirements Issues

Review current position descriptions and performance standards for accuracy.

Remember

Organize the work to be done. Review project outlines to identify discrete tasks and functions. Identify starting and ending times for tasks. As necessary, work with project schedules to maintain completion of deadlines.

As you do with employees who do not participate in the telework program, set clear expectations. Establish quantitative and qualitative goals for tasks and functions. Be clear what work is to be done, how much is to be completed, and when the work is due. Clarify each employee's role in ensuring successful results, especially of critical outcomes. Establish a procedure for addressing situations in which assignments are not completed properly or on time.

Consistent with performance management of employees not participating in the telework program, ensure the availability of necessary equipment. Determine the feasibility of procuring special equipment for designated employees or projects. Realign work assignments according to the availability of the required equipment.

Handbook for Managing Teleworkers – Toolkit

Improve Your Management Style

Remember — Strive to be comfortable supervising your employees without directly observing them. This requires that you be an effective communicator, establish and enforce clear standards of accountability, and be willing to negotiate through minor obstacles.

Seek training for managers and supervisors considering various telework programs.

Manage by objectives and results. Practice outlining the tasks and outcomes of a project. Clarify logical relationships and chronological dependencies. Highlight critical outcomes.

Focus on results, not processes. If you are uncomfortable managing employees in nontraditional work situations, confer with other managers who have more experience with such arrangements.

Be inclusive. Be sure to incorporate the opinions, guidance, or expertise of employees in a nontraditional work situation. Make sure you share important information with them in a timely manner.

If you have difficulty trusting your subordinates, give your employees the benefit of the doubt. Consider that "freedom to fail" is the necessary counterpart to "freedom to succeed."

Be flexible and open to new ideas. Consider that there may be multiple ways to achieve the same results. Ask for feedback from other managers and/or from your employees. Review statistics, best practices, and/or testimonials from other managers and supervisors on the success of nontraditional work situations.

Consider the benefits that come from telework programs:

☐ Lower attrition
☐ Increased ability to recruit and retain good employees
☐ Flexibility in balancing professional and personal priorities
☐ Enhanced job performance and motivation
☐ Improved morale
☐ Decreased stress

Success Stories

Automated Tracking Systems Enhance Accountability

For many years, government agencies relied on labor-intensive, manual tracking of telework participation. A new genre of automated systems allows for same-day response in accessing employee and/or historical telework records. As the Office of Personnel Management (OPM) and

Step One. Overcoming Management Resistance

Congress continue to require detailed reporting of telework implementation, automated tracking of data provides a quick, easy method for generating comprehensive and accurate responses.

The United States Department of Agriculture's (USDA) Telework Management System (TMS) is an excellent example of an effective automated tracking system. The TMS provides detailed information about teleworkers, including grade level, occupation, location, frequency, and type of telework, whether it is ad hoc or ongoing. In addition, the TMS automatically informs the IT staff of approved telework requests.

Susan Brown, the Telework Coordinator for USDA's Farm and Foreign Agricultural Services, said of the relatively new TMS system, "The IT department is notified by e-mail that the person has been approved for telework. Then the IT staff knows what equipment that person needs, since they know the type of telework the requestor will perform. The next version of the TMS will include the exact type of equipment each user requests."

The TMS has been in use since April 2006 and was developed in-house. Since that time, three USDA agencies have deployed it: Farm Service Agency, Foreign Agricultural Service, and Risk Management Agency.

Currently, there are 225 teleworkers in the system and 400 more will be added when the field offices fully implement the TMS. As an example of the resource savings to be realized by using the new system for tracking and reporting, the USDA Kansas City office had to manually count its data for the 2006 OPM Telework report.

"For Kansas City, data collection previously took two weeks, and then another two weeks to incorporate it into Washington's data. Soon, once Kansas is up and running with TMS, we'll just pull the report in less than a day," said Brown.

The good news is that the TMS is a system that could be easily employed by other Federal agencies.

"The TMS is definitely transferable. It is a Web-based system that is easily customizable for other agencies," said Brown. "The ability to quickly obtain data is a big relief and all the current information is input by employees."

Another example of an impressive telework tracking system is found at the International Trade Commission (ITC). The ITC was one of the first Federal agencies to develop an automated approach to requesting telework.

As Stephen McLaughlin, Director of Administration and CIO explained, "At first, you merely needed to request each telework instance by e-mail to the supervisor. For a year we maintained this 'easy' approval process, but it was hard to gather the necessary data for reporting annually to OPM.

The current system allows users to log in, enter their request, charge their time to the correct labor cost codes, add comments to provide greater detail about the individual telework arrangement, and notify the timekeeper and others along with their supervisor."

The information is maintained in a central database that can be readily accessed to produce the annual OPM telework report. "When you execute a telework agreement, you develop a teleworker profile in the system with all the relevant employee information. No more is there a staff person with 800 pieces of paper trying to figure out which grade level teleworked and for how many hours," said McLaughlin.

The ITC telework tracking system provides efficiency and accuracy in reporting that was unimaginable in the days of manual tracking. "It takes five minutes versus several weeks to derive data about teleworking. This task used to be time-consuming and resulted in horribly inaccurate information. I'm not sure how much we were not catching, but it was probably a lot. Now it's easy for teleworkers and management to understand our actual telework numbers. Incidents of 'underground' teleworking are almost nil now," said McLaughlin.

As with the USDA system, the ITC telework tracking system can be tailored for use by other government agencies. Furthermore, the ITC system has every teleworker in the system and has successfully been in use for more than two years.

The Defense Information Systems Agency (DISA) developed an automated tool that allows real-time tracking of applications with percentages of approvals, disapprovals, and pending requests. Management also can derive information about the number of employees in ad hoc or regular telework arrangements, and other relevant data that must be gathered in compliance with OPM's annual telework reporting requirements.

Aaron Glover, Special Assistant to the Director MPS (Manpower, Personnel, and Security), praised the developers of DISA's automated tool, which was designed and tested by members of DISA's internal Human Resources Systems Branch. "Not only was the project completed in less than 60 days, but the only cost to the organization was the labor of its developers," he said.

Glover offered insight on some of the benefits of the new system. "Employees now can submit applications for teleworking and get feedback almost instantly from their managers. DISA senior leadership now can view the status of the entire enterprise regarding employees' status on teleworking. This visibility is key to providing leaders the opportunity to recognize areas where resistance could exist and to take action to eliminate it."

Glover believes that the automated telework application is the cornerstone of DISA's success in expanding its telework program.

Source: *Keeping Telework on Track by Kathy Kadilak, Strategic WorkLife Solution, Teleworker, August 2007.*

Step One. Overcoming Management Resistance

Innovative Application of Technology To Support Telework

The United States Patent and Trademark Office (PTO), long recognized for its leadership in government telework program, entered a new phase in 2009 with the introduction of its Enterprise Remote Access (ERA) Portal. The portal was designed to extend telework as a versatile and economically-viable option by providing access to employee desktops and files through their own user-furnished equipment. Each portal user receives comprehensive pre-telework training and a PTO-supplied secure ID token for sanctioned network access.

Designed by the PTO's Office of the Chief Information Officer, the ERA Portal delivers an alternate solution to agency business units seeking to deploy safe, secure, and low to no-cost telework access for their eligible employees. Previously, PTO telework programs required government-furnished equipment (GFE) at an average cost of $2,800 per user. By contrast, the ERA Portal approach allows PTO operating units to deploy teleworkers with user-furnished equipment for as little as $105 per user.

The ERA Portal architecture relies on a secure socket layer (SSL) solution with a Virtual Private Network (VPN) via a Web portal. The software establishes a secure virtual environment on the remote client through which the teleworker accesses his/her office workstation through a Remote Desktop Protocol (RDP). At the time of initial connection, the remote client is checked for current anti-virus protection, which ensures the safety and security of PTO infrastructure and the integrity of government data.

Since the ERA Portal launch in early 2009, more than 350 PTO staff members have been trained and deployed to telework, an option not previously available to these employees. Further, the portal adoption has allowed the agency to avoid an estimated $980,000 that would have been associated with these deployments in the previous GFE-only model. A key component to the program's success to date is the mandatory training for each user that focuses on telework best practices, common questions, and essentials for secure remote operations – all of which combine to prepare employees to work from home within the agency's operating guidelines. The PTO CIO, John Owens, considers the portal a great new tool for our employees and allows them to use their own equipment to telework without incurring additional expenses by the agency. It has been a successful solution for our teleworkers and another means for the agency to meet its mission and business goals.

Step Two. Choosing Employees for Telework

Managers should learn or adjust methods of leading to ensure the continued success of telework, using existing quality and quantity work performance standards. Management for the teleworker should remain the same as for office employees and should measure performance by results without daily, direct observation. Along with being an effective communicator that clearly defines tasks and expectations, the manager should be supportive of telework and be willing to deal with any related minor problems or obstacles.

Matching Employees and Positions

Before a manager can consider a telework request, the manager and employee must examine the job requirements. While some jobs can be performed almost exclusively offsite, most jobs require a certain amount of time at the office. Jobs that require the worker to perform a daily, hands-on service for others are not adaptable to telework. **Must Do**

Positions Compatible for Telework

- ☐ Specific work activities are portable and can be performed as effectively outside the office
- ☐ Performance can be judged either through quality and timeliness of assignments or quantity of tasks completed or a combination of these factors
- ☐ An essential component of job responsibility consists of reading/processing tasks, e.g., reviewing case files, and writing legal briefs
- ☐ Face-to-face contact with other employees and clients is predictable or contact can be managed through telephone or e-mail communication
- ☐ Work planned for telework days is unclassified.
- ☐ The technology and equipment needed to perform the job offsite—such as use of a copier and fax machine—is available or can be adjusted for use on the days when the employee is in the primary office.
- ☐ The position adapts to cyclical work.
- ☐ Security and confidentiality of data, including sensitive, non-classified, Privacy Act information, can be adequately assured

Handbook for Managing Teleworkers – Toolkit

- ☐ Access to necessary reference materials is available through copying, faxing, or electronic transfer.
- ☐ Travel requirements for the position have been identified and anticipated. For example, trips may begin or end at the remote office rather than the main office and paperwork is accomplished at the remote office.

Eligible Employees

- ☐ The employee has demonstrated self-motivation, independence, and dependability in accomplishing work assignments.
- ☐ The employee can work effectively in an isolated environment.
- ☐ The employee has good time management skills.
- ☐ The employee's overall performance evaluations are high.
- ☐ The employee has clearly defined performance standards.
- ☐ The employee has satisfied satellite work station requirements, including availability of necessary equipment; privacy and lack of personal interruptions; security of sensitive, nonclassified data; and confidentiality of Privacy Act information.
- ☐ The employee has a history of reliable and responsible performance of duties in the current organization.
- ☐ The employee does not require close supervision or constant, face-to-face interaction with coworkers to complete assignments.

Determining Positions for Telework

! Must Do — The supervisor is responsible for deciding whether a position is appropriate for offsite work and for examining both the content of the work and the performance of the employee. If the manager believes the telework arrangement is not working (for example, the employee's performance declines or the participation interferes with organizational needs), he/she has the responsibility to end an employee's participation. However, a minimum of 90 days participation should be allowed to provide employees and supervisors a reasonable period of time to determine the viability of the telework arrangement. (The 90-day "trial" period is unnecessary for short-term, situational or project-based telework arrangements.)

Both the telecommuter and the supervisor need to remain adaptable, especially during the initial adjustment period. This flexibility will allow the teleworker to find the optimal arrangement for his/her personality and the job requirement.

By making the commitment to a telework program, employees and supervisors should remain flexible so they can respond to unexpected contingencies. Therefore, teleworkers must be able to:

- ☐ Work at the traditional worksite on telework days, when needed

Step Two. Choosing Employees for Telework

☐ Temporarily suspend telework, on an occasional basis, if necessitated by work requirements.

Conversely, requests by the employee to change his or her scheduled telework day in a particular week or biweekly pay period should be accommodated by the supervisor wherever practical, consistent with mission requirements.

Initiating Requests for Telework

> Employees wanting to be considered for telework should submit an initial request with information such as the telework schedule and location; any costs or cost savings to the government; and methods for avoiding disruption to the supervisor, coworkers, and clients. A cover memorandum explaining the reason for the request and any benefits to the government and the requester is optional. Depending upon who approves telework requests, the form is usually submitted to the first line supervisor for review and approval.
>
> *Tips*

Upon supervisory approval, the employee must complete the department's telework agreement form that covers the terms and conditions of the arrangement. This constitutes an agreement by the employee to adhere to applicable guidelines and policies. The telework agreement will cover items such as the voluntary nature and length of the telework arrangement; hours and days of duty for each work site; responsibilities for timekeeping, leave approval, and requests for overtime and compensatory time; performance requirements; proper use and safeguards of government property and records; and standards of conduct.

Selection Criteria

> Standardized selection criteria allows managers to objectively look at individuals rather than general categories. The primary goal is to ensure that a new participant has a good chance for success.
>
> *Tips*

Employee characteristics will probably be pretty much the same, whether they are in an office setting or offsite. For example, if an employee is an organized, efficient worker in the office he or she will most likely be the same way regardless of location. Likewise, if employees have poor work habits in the office the same difficulties will arise at the remote location. The following traits are indicative of whether someone might make an effective teleworker.

☐ Self-motivated and responsible
☐ Results oriented
☐ Independent worker
☐ Understands job requirements
☐ Understands agency policies and procedures
☐ Successful in current position
☐ Communicates well with supervisor, coworkers, and clients

Checklist

www.GovernmentTrainingInc.com

☐ Accepts change easily
☐ Interested in telecommuting

Checklist Also important are these work habits:
☐ Ability to set clear objectives
☐ Ability to clearly define tasks for the days teleworking
☐ Ability to schedule face-to-face interaction on specified days of the week
☐ Ability to meet internal and external needs while teleworking
☐ Ability to limit use of onsite stationary resources (both people and paper)
☐ Ability to control work schedule
☐ Ability to benefit from quiet or uninterrupted time.

Employee Assessment Questionnaire

The following questionnaire can be used as a guide for evaluating an employee's potential for successful telework. Rather than being a performance review or rating, it is an evaluation of individual work characteristics, habits, and competencies and an indicator of the likelihood of an employee's success.

Think through these questions carefully and answer them as fairly and objectively as possible.

After completing the questionnaire, discuss it with the employee. You may wish to give the employee a copy of the questionnaire in advance of this discussion. Once the discussion has taken place and agreement has been reached by both the employee and the manager as to the responses, copies of the completed questionnaire should be provided to the employee and placed in his or her file. This exercise can be performed on an annual basis or sooner if circumstances change.

Checklist **Employee Assessment Questionnaire**
Employee Name:_____
Employee Position: _____

1. Provide a brief summary of employee's duties and responsibilities.

2. Evaluate the following work characteristics according to the employee's existing job function (place a check under the appropriate column)

Clarity of goals and objectives for the position.	LOW	MEDIUM	HIGH
Ability to schedule face-to-face contact (meetings, etc.) on certain days of the week.	LOW	MEDIUM	HIGH

Step Two. Choosing Employees for Telework

Degree to which communications can be accomplished using voice mail, e-mail, faxing, electronic file transfer.	LOW	MEDIUM	HIGH
Ability to control work flow or schedule.	LOW	MEDIUM	HIGH
Reliability of technology to support employee when teleworking.	LOW	MEDIUM	HIGH

3. Evaluate the following work characteristics according to the employee's existing job function (place a check under the appropriate column).

Amount of in office face-to-face contact required.	LOW	MEDIUM	HIGH
Amount of in-office reference materials of other resources required.	LOW	MEDIUM	HIGH
Impact on work team when employee is teleworking.	LOW	MEDIUM	HIGH

4. Evaluate the employee's work style and level of performance characteristics (place a check under the appropriate column).

Level of job knowledge.	LOW	MEDIUM	HIGH
Experience on current assignment.	LOW	MEDIUM	HIGH
Level of organizing and planning skills.	LOW	MEDIUM	HIGH
Need for supervisor and/or frequent feedback.	LOW	MEDIUM	HIGH
Self-discipline regarding work.	LOW	MEDIUM	HIGH
Reliability concerning work hours.	LOW	MEDIUM	HIGH
Level of productivity.	LOW	MEDIUM	HIGH
Quality of work product.	LOW	MEDIUM	HIGH
Computer literacy.	LOW	MEDIUM	HIGH
Flexibility.	LOW	MEDIUM	HIGH

5. Evaluate the employee's work style and level of performance characteristics (place a check under the appropriate column).

Resistance to change.	LOW	MEDIUM	HIGH
Need for interpersonal office contact	LOW	MEDIUM	HIGH
Importance of co-worker input to successful job performance.	LOW	MEDIUM	HIGH

6. Does this employee work with information, data or materials requiring secure or special handling?
YES_____ NO_____

7. Rate your willingness to let this employee participate in VRS.

_____ Not willing

_____ Have reservations (but willing)

_____ Completely willing

8. If you indicated the first or second option above, please state your reasons below.

_____ _____

Supervisor's Signature Date

_____ _____

www.GovernmentTrainingInc.com

Employee's Acknowledgement Date

NOTE:

Q2. If your responses were primarily in the medium to high columns, this employee is likely to be a successful teleworker.

Q3 If your responses were primarily in the low to medium columns, this employee is likely to be a successful teleworker.

Q4. Your response ratings to the questions above depend on the critical nature of the work style and performance characteristics of the employee's existing job. If your responses were primarily in the medium to high columns, this employee is likely to be a successful teleworker.

Q5. If your responses were primarily in the low to medium columns, this employee is likely to be a successful teleworker.

Profiling Teleworkers

By allowing an employee to take advantage of telework, you are empowering that person and trusting that he or she will do a good job. Such proposals should be decided on a case-by-case basis, because each job situation and employee is different—and because your style and preferences as a manager are important too.

The following three profiles – for job requirements, employee success, and management – will help you make this determination. In each profile, rate eight criteria according to how frequently they are present—on a scale from "Always" to "Never." At the end of the three profiles is a summary that provides an overview of the responses given.

This tool only provides an initial indication whether the job responsibilities can be successfully met by the employee and should be only one aspect of your overall decision. Your final determination should balance employees' needs with the requirements of the job and the demands of the department's mission, while taking your management style into consideration as well.

Part 1: Job Requirements Profile

Checklist

Tasks and Functions Are Distinct or Readily Defined

☐ Always   ☐ Most of the Time   ☐ About Half the Time   ☐ Rarely   ☐ Never

Work Can Be Scheduled or Time Controlled

☐ Always   ☐ Most of the Time   ☐ About Half the Time   ☐ Rarely   ☐ Never

Quantity and Quality of Work Are Measurable

☐ Always   ☐ Most of the Time   ☐ About Half the Time   ☐ Rarely   ☐ Never

Quality of Worker's Performance Can Remain High

☐ Always   ☐ Most of the Time   ☐ About Half the Time   ☐ Rarely   ☐ Never

Step Two. Choosing Employees for Telework

Quality of Colleagues' Performance Can Remain High

☐ Always ☐ Most of the Time ☐ About Half the Time ☐ Rarely ☐ Never

Quality of Customer Service Can Remain High

☐ Always ☐ Most of the Time ☐ About Half the Time ☐ Rarely ☐ Never

Can Be Performed without Special Equipment

☐ Always ☐ Most of the Time ☐ About Half the Time ☐ Rarely ☐ Never

Can Be Performed by Other Staff on a Back-Up Basis

Part 2: Employee Success Profile

Performs at or above Expected Levels

☐ Always ☐ Most of the Time ☐ About Half the Time ☐ Rarely ☐ Never

Understands Job Responsibilities

☐ Always ☐ Most of the Time ☐ About Half the Time ☐ Rarely ☐ Never

Works Well Independently

☐ Always ☐ Most of the Time ☐ About Half the Time ☐ Rarely ☐ Never

Reliable and Accountable

☐ Always ☐ Most of the Time ☐ About Half the Time ☐ Rarely ☐ Never

Communicates Well

☐ Always ☐ Most of the Time ☐ About Half the Time ☐ Rarely ☐ Never

Maintains Good Relationships with Peers and Customers

☐ Always ☐ Most of the Time ☐ About Half the Time ☐ Rarely ☐ Never

Organizes Work Well, Including Multiple Assignments

☐ Always ☐ Most of the Time ☐ About Half the Time ☐ Rarely ☐ Never

Flexible

☐ Always ☐ Most of the Time ☐ About Half the Time ☐ Rarely ☐ Never

Part 3: Management Profile

Manages by Objectives and Results

☐ Always ☐ Most of the Time ☐ About Half the Time ☐ Rarely ☐ Never

Comfortable Managing Nontraditional Work Situations

☐ Always ☐ Most of the Time ☐ About Half the Time ☐ Rarely ☐ Never

Flexible

☐ Always ☐ Most of the Time ☐ About Half the Time ☐ Rarely ☐ Never

Communicates Well

☐ Always ☐ Most of the Time ☐ About Half the Time ☐ Rarely ☐ Never

Provides Coaching

☐ Always ☐ Most of the Time ☐ About Half the Time ☐ Rarely ☐ Never

Able To Trust Subordinates

☐ Always ☐ Most of the Time ☐ About Half the Time ☐ Rarely ☐ Never

Promotes Empowerment

☐ Always ☐ Most of the Time ☐ About Half the Time ☐ Rarely ☐ Never

Open to New Ideas

☐ Always ☐ Most of the Time ☐ About Half the Time ☐ Rarely ☐ Never

Part1: Job Requirements

Tasks and Functions Are Distinct and Readily Defined

☐ Do tasks have clear beginning and end points?

Work Can Be Scheduled or Time Controlled

☐ Can work be assigned for particular days of the week? Can work be accomplished within a set time frame with clear deadlines?

Quantity and Quality of Work Are Measurable

☐ Can you track the amount of work produced? Can you easily assess the quality of the work performed?

Quality of Worker's Performance Can Remain High

☐ Will the proposed job arrangement enable the worker to perform as well or better than he/she does now?

Quality of Colleagues' Performance Can Remain High

☐ Can the work be accomplished without substantial face-to-face interaction with others? Will the proposed job arrangement enable the worker's colleagues to perform as well or better than they do now?

Quality of Customer Service Can Remain High

☐ Will the proposed job arrangement enable the worker to serve customers as well or better than he/she does now? Is face-to-face interaction with customers routinely required?

Can Be Performed without Special Equipment

☐ Can the work be accomplished with equipment that is normally found in most work environments?

Step Two. Choosing Employees for Telework

Can Be Performed by Other Staff on a Back-up Basis
☐ Are other staff trained and available to perform this job function whenever necessary?

Part 2: Employee Success Profile

Performs at or above Expected Levels
☐ Has your employee done satisfactory work on a consistent basis?

Understands Job Responsibilities
☐ Does your employee understand his/her roles and responsibilities within your office? Does he/she understand how his/her work and productivity impact others and the agency's mission?

Works Well Independently
☐ Do you have to constantly request information from or give direction to your employee? Does your employee work well independently and produce high-quality work without frequent supervision?

Reliable and Accountable
☐ Is your employee reliable? Do you trust him/her to get the job done? Does he/she consistently follow up? Does he/she take initiative to address and overcome challenges?

Communicates Well
☐ Do you keep your employees informed about the status of assignments, projects, and work issues? Do you clearly and consistently communicate your expectations of employee performance? Do you give clear and consistent feedback to employees on their performance?

Maintains Good Relationships with Peers and Customers
☐ Does your employee have good relationships with peers, customers, and team members? Will he/she be able to accomplish team assignments and inter-agency projects?

Organizes Work Well, Including Multiple Assignments
☐ Is your employee well organized? Is he/she able to set priorities and accomplish work efficiently? Is he/she able to work on several assignments simultaneously?

Flexible
☐ Is your employee flexible? Has he/she been willing to take on new assignments? Is he/she willing to switch scheduled workdays if necessary or adjust his/her work schedule?

Part 3: Management Profile

Manages by Objectives and Results
☐ Do you provide employees with clear direction on the tasks to be performed and the results you expect?

Comfortable Managing Nontraditional Work Situations
☐ Do you keep your employees informed about the status of assignments, projects, and work issues? Do you clearly and consistently communicate your expectations of employee performance? Do you give clear and consistent feedback to employees on their performance?

Flexible
☐ Are you able to be flexible in the face of changing circumstances or work arrangements?

Communicates Well
☐ Do you keep your employees informed about the status of assignments, projects, and work issues? Do you clearly and consistently communicate your expectations of employee performance? Do you give clear and consistent feedback to employees on their performance?

Provides Coaching
☐ Do you assist employees in building their skills and competencies? Do you coach them on areas they need to improve upon and/or provide them with training opportunities?

Able To Trust Subordinates
☐ Do you believe that employees in nontraditional work situations will be responsible in the performance of their duties?

Promotes Empowerment
☐ Are you able to give your employees the freedom to work on their own and/or to manage their own work schedules? Do you believe that opportunities to use nontraditional work situations will contribute to your employees' growth and development?

Open to New Ideas
☐ Are you open to considering different ways to get a job done as long as it is successfully completed?

Step Two. Choosing Employees for Telework

Workers With Disabilities

> One of the best potential sources of teleworkers can be found among workers with disabilities. However, not all persons with disabilities need - or want - to work at home. And not all jobs can be performed at home. But allowing an employee to work at home may be a reasonable accommodation where the person's disability prevents successfully performing the job onsite and the job, or parts of the job, can be performed at home without causing significant difficulty or expense.

Remember

In July 2010, President Barack Obama issued an executive order instructing Federal agencies to increase employment of people with disabilities. The directive orders agencies to take steps to meet a goal of hiring an additional 100,000 disabled employees over five years that was originally laid out by President Clinton in a July 2000 executive order. "Few steps were taken to implement that executive order in subsequent years," said Obama. "As the nation's largest employer, the Federal government must become a model for the employment of individuals with disabilities. Executive departments and agencies must improve their efforts to employ workers with disabilities through increased recruitment, hiring and retention of these individuals."

According to the executive order, approximately 54 million Americans are living with disabilities. Obama said the Federal government has an important interest in reducing discrimination against such Americans, in eliminating the stigma associated with disability and in encouraging Americans with disabilities to seek employment in the Federal workforce.

The order directs the head of the Office of Personnel Management (OPM), in consultation with the Labor secretary, the chair of the EEOC, and the director of the Office of Management and Budget, to design strategies for recruiting and hiring people with disabilities within 60 days. The OPM director also must develop mandatory training programs for agency human resources personnel and hiring managers on the employment of people with disabilities.

Agencies will then be required to develop their own plans for promoting employment opportunities for disabled individuals. The plans, to be spearheaded by senior-level officials, must include performance targets and numerical goals.

In implementing their plans, agencies are expected to increase their use of Schedule A excepted service hiring authority and to increase participation of people with disabilities in internships, fellowships and training and mentoring programs. Agencies must report frequently on their progress in implementing their plans. Their reports will be published on OPM's website.

In addition to the hiring initiatives, the order requires agencies to take steps to improve retention of disabled workers. Among strategies available to them, according to the order, are improved training, the use of centralized funds to provide reasonable accommodations, increased access to accessible technologies, and ensuring the accessibility of physical and virtual workspaces.

Also, Obama ordered that "agencies shall make special efforts, to the extent permitted by law, to ensure the retention of those who are injured on the job. Agencies shall work to improve, expand, and increase successful return-to-work outcomes for those of their employees who sustain work-related injuries and illnesses, as defined under the Federal Employees' Compensation Act, by increasing the availability of job accommodations and light or limited duty jobs, removing disincentives for FECA claimants to return to work, and taking other appropriate measures."

Under the executive order, the Labor secretary must pursue "innovative re-employment strategies" that increase the likelihood of an injured employee returning to work, including by pursuing reform of the FECA system.

Americans with Disabilities Act

In its 1999 Enforcement Guidance on Reasonable Accommodation and Undue Hardship Under the Americans with Disabilities Act (revised 10/17/02), the Equal Employment Opportunity Commission said that allowing an individual with a disability to work at home may be a form of reasonable accommodation. The Americans with Disabilities Act (ADA) requires employers with 15 or more employees to provide reasonable accommodation for qualified applicants and employees with disabilities. Reasonable accommodation is any change in the work environment or in the way things are customarily done that enables an individual with a disability to apply for a job, perform a job, or gain equal access to the benefits and privileges of a job. The ADA does not require an employer to provide a specific accommodation if it causes undue hardship, such as significant difficulty or expense. Follows are some commonly asked questions (and answers) about the ADA and telework.

Does the ADA require employers to have telework programs?

No. The ADA does not require an employer to offer a telework program to all employees. However, if an employer does offer telework, it must allow employees with disabilities an equal opportunity to participate in such a program.

In addition, the ADA's reasonable accommodation obligation, which includes modifying workplace policies, might require an employer to waive certain eligibility requirements or otherwise modify its telework program for someone with a disability who needs to work at home. For example, an employer may generally require that employees work at least one year before they are eligible to participate in a telework program. If a new employee needs to work at home because of a disability, and the job can be performed at home, then an employer may have to waive its one-year rule for this individual.

Step Two. Choosing Employees for Telework

May permitting an employee to work at home be a reasonable accommodation, even if the employer has no telework program?

Yes. Changing the location where work is performed may fall under the ADA's reasonable accommodation requirement of modifying workplace policies, even if the employer does not allow other employees to telework. However, an employer is not obligated to adopt an employee's preferred or requested accommodation and may instead offer alternate accommodations as long as they would be effective. (See Question 6.)

How should an employer determine whether someone may need to work at home as a reasonable accommodation?

This determination should be made through a flexible "interactive process" between the employer and the individual. The process begins with a request. An individual must first inform the employer that the medical condition requires some change in the way the job is performed. The individual does not need to use special words, such as "ADA" or "reasonable accommodation" to make this request, but must let the employer know that a medical condition interferes with his/her ability to do the job.

Then the employer and the individual need to discuss the person's request so that the employer understands why the disability might necessitate the individual working at home. The individual must explain what limitations from the disability make it difficult to do the job in the workplace, and how the job could still be performed from the employee's home. The employer may request information about the individual's medical condition (including reasonable documentation) if it is unclear whether it is a "disability" as defined by the ADA. The employer and employee may wish to discuss other types of accommodations that would allow the person to remain full-time in the workplace. However, in some situations, working at home may be the only effective option for an employee with a disability.

Tips

How should an employer determine whether a particular job can be performed at home?

An employer and employee first need to identify and review all of the essential job functions. The essential functions or duties are those tasks that are fundamental to performing a specific job. An employer does not have to remove any essential job duties to permit an employee to work at home. However, it may need to reassign some minor job duties or marginal functions (such as those that are nonessential to the successful performance of a job) if they cannot be performed outside the workplace and they are the only obstacle to permitting an employee to work at home. If a marginal function needs to be reassigned, an employer may substitute another minor task that the employee with a disability could perform at home in order to keep employee workloads evenly distributed.

After determining what functions are essential, the employer and the individual with a disability should determine whether some or all of the functions can be performed at home. For some jobs, the essential duties can only be performed in the workplace. For example, food servers, cashiers,

www.GovernmentTrainingInc.com

and truck drivers cannot perform their essential duties from home. But, in many other jobs some or all of the duties can be performed at home.

Remember: Several factors should be considered in determining the feasibility of working at home, including the employer's ability to supervise the employee adequately and whether any duties require use of certain equipment or tools that cannot be replicated at home. Other critical considerations include whether there is a need for face-to-face interaction and coordination of work with other employees; whether in-person interaction with outside colleagues, clients, or customers is necessary; and whether the position in question requires the employee to have immediate access to documents or other information located only in the workplace. An employer should not, however, deny a request to work at home as a reasonable accommodation solely because a job involves some contact and coordination with other employees. Frequently, meetings can be conducted effectively by telephone and information can be exchanged quickly through e-mail.

If the employer determines that some job duties must be performed in the workplace, then the employer and employee need to decide whether working part-time at home and part-time in the workplace will meet both of their needs. For example, an employee may need to meet face-to-face with clients as part of a job, but other tasks may involve reviewing documents and writing reports. Clearly, the meetings must be done in the workplace, but the employee may be able to review documents and write reports from home.

How frequently may someone with a disability work at home as a reasonable accommodation?

An employee may work at home only to the extent that his/her disability necessitates it. For some people, that may mean one day a week, two half-days, or every day for a particular period of time (for example, for three months while an employee recovers from treatment or surgery related to a disability). In other instances, the nature of a disability may make it difficult to predict precisely when it will be necessary for an employee to work at home. For example, sometimes the effects of a disability become particularly severe on a periodic but irregular basis. When these flare-ups occur, they sometimes prevent an individual from getting to the workplace. In these instances, an employee might need to work at home on an "as needed" basis, if this can be done without undue hardship.

As part of the interactive process, the employer should discuss with the individual whether the disability necessitates working at home full-time or part-time. (Some individuals may only be able to perform their jobs successfully by working at home full time.) If the disability necessitates working at home part-time, then the employer and employee should develop a schedule that meets both of their needs. Both the employer and the employee should be flexible in working out a schedule so that work is done in a timely way, since an employer does not have to lower production standards for individuals with disabilities who are working at home. The employer and employee also need to discuss how the employee will be supervised.

Step Two. Choosing Employees for Telework

May an employer make accommodations that enable an employee to work full-time in the workplace rather than granting a request to work at home?

Yes, the employer may select any effective accommodation, even if it is not the one preferred by the employee. Reasonable accommodations include adjustments or changes to the workplace, such as: providing devices or modifying equipment, making workplaces accessible (e.g., installing a ramp), restructuring jobs, modifying work schedules and policies, and providing qualified readers or sign language interpreters. An employer can provide any of these types of reasonable accommodations, or a combination of them, to permit an employee to remain in the workplace. For example, an employee with a disability who needs to use paratransit asks to work at home because the paratransit schedule does not permit the employee to arrive before 10 a.m., two hours after the normal starting time. An employer may allow the employee to begin his or her eight-hour shift at 10a.m., rather than granting the request to work at home, if this would work with the paratransit schedule.

How can employers and individuals with disabilities learn more about reasonable accommodation, including working at home?

Employers and individuals with disabilities wishing to learn more about working at home as a reasonable accommodation can contact the EEOC at (202) 663-4691, (202) 663-4691 (voice) and (202) 663-7026, (202) 663-7026 (TTY). General information about reasonable accommodation can be found on EEOC's website, *www.eeoc.gov/policy/guidance.html* (Enforcement Guidance on Reasonable Accommodation and Undue Hardship Under the Americans with Disabilities Act; revised 10/17/02). This website also provides guidance on many other aspects of the ADA.

The government-funded Job Accommodation Network (JAN) is a free service that offers employers and individuals ideas about effective accommodations. The counselors perform individualized searches for workplace accommodations based on a job's functional requirements, the functional limitations of the individual, environmental factors, and other pertinent information. *JAN can be reached at 800-526-7234, 800-526-7234 (voice or TDD); or at www.jan.wvu.edu/soar.*

Unnecessary Barriers: A Report on Federal Employment of Americans with Disabilities
Background: Employees with disabilities are leaving the Federal workforce at nearly twice the rate of their hire[3]. In September, President Obama stated, "…the Federal government and its contractors can lead the way by implementing effective employment policies and practices that increase opportunities and help workers [with disabilities] achieve their full potential.[4]" Fifty-four percent of people age 21-64 with some type of disability were unemployed in the past year.[5] Yet, just 1 percent of Federal positions are currently held by an employee with a disability. The Report on Federal Employment of Americans with Disabilities explores how

---

3 The National Council on Disability's Federal Employment of People With Disabilities Report, March 31, 2009
4 http://www.whitehouse.gov/the_press_office/Presidential-Proclamation-National-Disability-Employment-Awareness-Month
5 http://www.census.gov/Press-Release/www/releases/archives/facts_for_features_special_editions/013739.html

agencies are hiring, managing, and retaining employees with disabilities – and identifies the opportunity for advancement.

Methodology: Telework Exchange, in partnership with the Federal Managers Association, conducted an online survey between January 25, 2010 and February 5, 2010 of 513 Federal government employees involved in the hiring or management process. Thirty-one percent of those surveyed work in Department of Defense agencies and 69 percent work in Federal civilian agencies; 45 percent are directly involved in researching or evaluating accommodations[6] for employees with disabilities. The sample size results in a margin of error of +/- 4.27 percent at a 95 percent confidence level.

Key Findings:

Seventy-one percent of Federal employees[7] report their agency is committed to hiring employees with disabilities

However, just half say their agency has the knowledge and tools needed to hire, retain, and promote employees with disabilities

While 84 percent of respondents believe their agency offers "reasonable accommodations" to employees with disabilities, just half say their agency offers telework or technical support options[8], and less than a quarter offer job share options or personal-care assistance

Fifty-four percent of employees, who work at agencies without proper tools and knowledge, admit they are not adequately prepared to provide accommodations

Unnecessary barriers to recruiting and retaining employees with disabilities include:

- Lack of education about key mandates – 36 percent of Federal employees involved in approving or authorizing new hires or promotions are not familiar[9] with Schedule A[10] and 58 percent are not familiar with Executive Order 13163[11]

- Lack of manager training – 40 percent of Federal managers have not received adequate training to effectively manage employees with disabilities and 45 percent have not received adequate training to effectively retain employees with disabilities. Half of Federal employees say managers' lack of training is a significant barrier to recruiting and retaining employees with disabilities in their agency

- Lack of accountability – 46 percent of employees say their agency is not monitoring, or they are unsure if they are monitoring progress related to the hiring, advancement, and/or retention of employees with disabilities. Forty-four percent don't know who is responsible for decisions related to the hiring, advancement, and/or retention of employees with disabilities in their agency

Though stereotypes are also a barrier, they are significantly less common in agencies with proper tools and knowledge

---

6   For the purpose of this research, we define "accommodations" for employees with disabilities to be physical, access, communications, and technology support
7   Employees involved in hiring/management
8   With a focus on persons with disabilities
9   Not very or not at all familiar
10 http://www.dotcr.ost.dot.gov/asp/pwdfaq.asp#6
11 http://frwebgate.access.gpo.gov/cgi-bin/getdoc.cgi?dbname=2000_register&docid=fr28jy00-139.pdf

Step Two. Choosing Employees for Telework

Additionally, agencies with committed senior management[12] are significantly more likely to train employees adequately, provide needed technical support, and monitor progress related to the hiring, advancement, and/or retention of employees with disabilities

Recommendations:

Accommodations alone will not enable Americans with disabilities to reach their full potential in the Federal workforce. Agencies must focus on:

- Management:
- Secure management commitment
- Monitor agency progress related to the hiring, advancement, and retention of employees with disabilities

Education:

Train hiring and program managers on recruiting, managing, and retaining employees with disabilities

Educate on key mandates and advocate for equal opportunity

Equipment:

Offer improved physical, access, communications, and technical accommodations

For more information on the Unnecessary Barriers report or Telework Exchange, please contact Erin Lundberg at (301) 785-0004 or elundberg@teleworkexchange.com.

Source: Telework Exchange

From Office Worker To Teleworker

After gaining approval to begin telework managing, managers need to do the following:

☐ Complete the application form and submit it to your supervisor.

☐ Complete the Employee Assessment Questionnaire.

☐ Discuss the results of the Employee Assessment Questionnaire.

☐ Determine the parameters you will follow when meeting with your teleworkers.

☐ Reach agreement on their hours of work, days out of the office, days in the office, etc.

☐ Complete the program work agreement (agreement) and the safety/security checklist for your teleworkers.

☐ Make arrangements for high-speed telecommunication service to be installed for your teleworkers.

☐ Ensure teleworkers complete the training course designed for the program.

☐ While waiting for high-speed telecommunication service, begin a trial period under the parameters set forth in the agreement.

☐ Assess the outcome of the trial period and determine if any changes to the Agreement are necessary.

---

[12] Committed senior management were rated 6-10 on a scale of 1-10 with 1 being not at all committed to hiring employees with disabilities and 10 being completely committed

www.GovernmentTrainingInc.com

How Workers' Compensation Works For Teleworkers

One of the biggest questions posed by teleworkers and their managers concerns workers' compensation. Teleworkers are covered by the Federal Tort Claims Act or the Federal Employees Compensation Act (FECA) and qualify for continuation of pay or workers' compensation for on-the-job injury or occupational illness. When reviewing workers' compensation cases, consider the following:

- The supervisor's signature on the request for compensation attests only to what the supervisor can reasonably know whether the event occurred at a conventional work site or at an alternative work site (e.g., home) during official duty.

- Under normal circumstances, supervisors are often not present when an employee sustains an injury.

Employees, in all situations, bear responsibility for informing their immediate supervisor of an injury at the earliest time possible. They must also provide details to the Department of Labor when filing a claim.

The Federal equivalent of workers' compensation limits recovery by an employee injured while on duty to reasonable amounts. Supervisors must ensure that claims of this type are brought to the attention of the servicing personnel office.

The supervisor must also require the employee to designate one area in the home as the official workstation. The government's potential exposure to liability could possibly then be restricted to that one area.

Telework arrangements can also help to put injured employees back to work and off the compensation rolls. Organizations may wish to determine which employees currently on the compensation rolls might be able to perform some portion of their work at home. Accommodations of special equipment or restructuring assignments may enable an employee to resume work and terminate worker's compensation.

The Appeals Process

Your employee has submitted an application for participation and you have determined he/she is not suited for working from a remote environment.

You have completed the assessment sheet and discussed your misgivings with the employee, but the two of you cannot come to agreement. Now what?

The manager has the final word on whether an employee can work from an alternate worksite. The employee, however, does have appeal rights, which are as follows:

- ☐ Meet a second time with the employee to try to reach agreement on the matter.
- ☐ If agreement cannot be reached, advise the employee that he/she has the right to appeal your decision to his/her next level manager, and how to go about it.
- ☐ Advise the employee the appeal must be in writing (e-mail is acceptable) and must be received by the manager within five (5) workdays.
- ☐ If the employee indicates that he/she appeals your decision, schedule a meeting to be attended by you, your manager, and the employee.
- ☐ Allow sufficient time for your manager to listen to both points of view.

Step Two. Choosing Employees for Telework

- ☐ Discuss with your manager the background and history of why this meeting is necessary.
- ☐ Bring any documentation to the meeting supporting your position and advise the employee to do the same.
- ☐ Present your "case" to your manager.
- ☐ Allow the employee sufficient time to present his/her "case".
- ☐ Answer any questions posed by your manager and/or the employee.
- ☐ Allow your manager reasonable time to make his/her decision.
- ☐ The second level manager's decision is final.

Performance Management From A Distance

Performance management in the Federal government is difficult from any aspect, yet managing from a distance can be even more challenging. The manager's role must evolve into the role of "coach or facilitator" rather than "enforcer". This means that rather than overseeing behavior the manager of a teleworker must oversee outputs.

Here are some basic points for dealing with performance problems with remote employees:
- ☐ Provide a clear and specific performance plan.
- ☐ Provide notice that the employee is performing at an unacceptable level in one or more elements.
- ☐ Provide counseling and assistance in an effort to improve performance.
- ☐ Provide a notice of proposed adverse action.
- ☐ Make a final decision.

Tips

Step Four will provide information on developing and building trust and mentoring, in hopes of avoiding performance problems and related issues.

Success Stories

Creating A Telework-Friendly Environment

With more than 10,000 employees nationwide, the Centers for Disease Control & Prevention (CDC) recognized a need to create a more telework-friendly operating environment and took steps to support remote workforce options during the past year. With essential senior leadership support, the enterprise-wide telework program has been organized like any other major initiative, with a ranking program manager empowered to develop and implement policies and procedures that encourage telework participation across the organization. The CDC goals for the program parallel the agency mission: focus on delivering timely and accurate critical information to the public, manage and contain costs, and maintain a skilled, satisfied workforce.

Under the Telework Improvement Initiative, the CDC:

- ☐ Increased telework participation from 18 percent of eligible employees to 30 percent during the last 12 months
- ☐ Conducted a comprehensive employee eligibility determination for more than 7,000 employees based on job function
- ☐ Ensured all teleworkers and their supervisors participated in updated telework training
- ☐ Purchased 1,900+ additional laptops to be used solely by teleworkers, and a distribution strategy was implemented to ensure that no one was denied the privilege to telework based solely on lack of funding
- ☐ Developed a Telework Management System, which facilitates electronic routing and authorization of telework requests/agreements
- ☐ Developed an internal Telework Web portal, which serves as the single repository for all telework related news, policies, and forms

Customer surveys indicate service levels were preserved or improved, regardless of where the CDC staff worked during the evaluation period. By making telework a strategic priority for the CDC, the agency demonstrated its commitment to quality of service, while supporting employee work-life balance. Further, as it is mandatory that the CDC be able to continue to function in a reliable, business-like manner during public health emergencies, the telework expansion program is directly linked to the agency mission accomplishment. Not insignificantly, the agency also has realized tangible cost-savings by maximizing office hoteling, as well as space and equipment sharing models that have combined to reduce overall operating budgets. CDC officials credit their success to the involvement of all stakeholders in the planning and implementation of the telework program, which has made this a collaborative, joint success for employees, supervisors, senior leadership, and organized labor groups.

Telework Program With Maximum Impact On Government

The Software Protection Initiative from the U.S. Air Force Research Laboratory offers a free, telework-friendly, portable tool that provides a safer, local environment for connecting to any network or cloud computing application. Lightweight Portable Security (LPS) creates a non-persistent computing environment from a mini-CD. LPS comes in two editions: LPS-Public for general browsing and the more secure LPS-Remote Access customized to access only your organization's network.

LPS is Government Off the Shelf (GOTS) software that is trustworthy, extremely deployable, and easily maintained. Its simplicity lends itself to supporting teleworkers with minimal helpdesk support and its flexibility enables operations of mobile workers in unpredictable environments, including humanitarian and disaster relief missions. This innovative technology turns almost

Step Two. Choosing Employees for Telework

any x86 computer (Mac, Windows, or Linux) into a temporarily trusted system for safe Internet browsing and secure network access. Booting Linux from a LiveCD and installing nothing, LPS runs in RAM and does not mount the hard drive thus bypassing local malware. LPS's various editions will remain free as SPI's budget/resources allow.

Each LPS edition serves a specific use, focusing on the task to be performed and the requisite security. The free LPS-Public edition provides a safe, easy way to browse the Internet, access Department of Defense (DoD) Common Access Card (CAC)-enabled Web sites, and connect to remote networks without leaving a trace. To date, the U.S. Air Force has distributed more than 38,000 copies of LPS-Public. Download the software at *http://spi.dod.mil/lipose.htm*.

The LPS-Remote Access edition provides very secure remote desktop access from an exceptionally locked-down operating system (OS) that may only connect to pre-specified organization's resources. It's customized to match your existing infrastructure and organizational needs. LPS technology was conceived in 2001 but the 2009 H1N1 pandemic threat drove the creation of LPS-Remote Access and its accreditation as a Continuity of Operations (COOP) solution. The software has been evaluated by the National Security Agency and was approved for DoD-wide emergency telework use by the DoD Chief Information Officer in December 2009. It's the only approved means to allow non-government-furnished (e.g. private or public) computers to connect to the DoD's Unclassified but Sensitive Internet Protocol Router Network (NIPRNet).

LPS-Remote Access was deemed by the DoD as the easiest and least expensive telework solution for its geographically-dispersed workforce. Deployment entailed burning and distributing free CDs and inexpensive smartcard-readers to users, rather than having to issue and update government laptops or requiring users to install specialized software on their personal computing devices. LPS-Remote Access customization and Tier 2 support is available for all Federal agencies and many of their contractors. More than 30 organizations representing some 30,000 government employees have adopted LPS-Remote Access. To learn more and request a build, visit *https://spi.dod.mil/COOP/DoD_reg_SSL.htm*.

Workplace Works For The State Of Minnesota

In 2009, the Minnesota Department of Transportation sponsored and developed the eWorkPlace initiative to reduce congestion in the Twin Cities of Minneapolis and St. Paul. The program, which encourages local employers to offer a telework option, to date has 30 employers enrolled, representing more than 2,400 teleworking participants. The companies involved have reported significant cost-savings, increased recruitment and retention rates, and productivity increases attributed to the eWorkPlace initiative. Simultaneously, their employees benefit from reduced commuting time, aggravation, and cost, and report increased job satisfaction with more improved work-life balance.

To ensure lasting results, eWorkPlace provides employees and employers with access to a free and secure online Commute Tool to evaluate their potential reduction of vehicle miles travelled and emissions, as well as time and money saved by teleworking. It offers options to survey participants, gauges who is using the program, and can provide employers with feedback about how well their employees like teleworking.

After the first year, eWorkPlace participants agree that teleworking employees are more engaged and productive – as evidenced by one CEO's comment, "A major advantage of our telework strategy is the loyalty and commitment of our customer representatives. The convenience and flexibility of their jobs has kept our turnover minimal." In addition, managers and employees from multiple organizations report they are experiencing less stress, better well-being, higher expectations, and improved interpersonal relationships.

This is a program that can work for most communities and reduces greenhouse gas emissions. A Carver County, MN Commissioner noted, "Less commuting for our residents means more people running errands, eating lunch and shopping right here in our community rather than at businesses near their far-away workplaces. We see it as a potential boost to our County's economic health, which might be coming at a perfect time for many of our small businesses."

Outstanding Telework Managers

Federal: Danette Campbell, Senior Telework Advisor, United States Patent and Trademark Office

Ms. Danette Campbell is the Senior Telework Advisor for the United States Patent and Trademark Office (PTO), part of the Department of Commerce (DOC). She represents the PTO on telework-related matters and oversees the agency's enterprise-wide telework program. Since Ms. Campbell joined the PTO in 2006, the number of employees teleworking on a regular basis has nearly doubled to more than 5,500 participants in 2010. She helped establish a successful office hoteling program, which has allowed the PTO to avoid expenditure of an estimated $11 million in additional real estate expense. Equally important, and in direct support of the agency mission – the expanded telework initiatives have allowed the PTO to continue hiring patent examiners, without incurring additional office space.

In addition to educating managers on telework strategies and providing telework training, Ms. Campbell helps the PTO business units design, develop, and refine their individual telework initiatives. She works closely with the Chief Information Officer, the Chief Administrative Officer, and other stakeholders to report telework program progress and to ensure teleworking technology requirements are met. Ms. Campbell is focused on internal and external communications by maintaining an internal telework resource Web site and by frequently meeting with other agencies and organizations to promote telework and share best practices.

Step Two. Choosing Employees for Telework

Ms. Campbell is a recognized voice and leader in the Federal telework community. She is known for her tenacity, attention to detail, and commitment to expanding telework for the Federal workforce. Her many achievements and proven success within the PTO demonstrates her remarkable abilities to lead strategic programs, champion executive support, and collaborate with stakeholders inside and outside of the organization to continue momentum for government-wide telework initiatives.

State: Janie E. Bowen, Virginia Tax Commissioner, Virginia Department of Taxation

As the Virginia Tax Commissioner, Ms. Janie Bowen is directly responsible for the operation and management of the Virginia Department of Taxation. She is focused on the agency's mission to collect and deposit taxes, administer the tax laws for individuals and corporations doing business in Virginia, and she advises the Governor and General Assembly on tax policy and operations.

Ms. Bowen also has been a leading proponent for building a robust, innovative, and pragmatic telework program at the Department of Taxation. She initiated a top-down approach with buy-in from agency executives and managers before she engaged the broader staff in this transformational process. She founded the telework program with an emphasis on improving the agency's performance, named a telework program manager, and encouraged a phased and staged implementation strategy with feedback and improvement opportunities throughout the agency-wide roll-out. The success of the Tax Department's telework program has attracted the interest of other Virginia state agencies, and Ms. Bowen continues to be an experienced advocate for expanded telework across government.

To date, more than 60 percent of the Department of Taxation's nearly 700 teleworking employees work from home one day a week, and 382 are permanently home-based. As one of the leading telework programs among public and private employers in the Commonwealth, the Virginia Department of Taxation is a model for other organizations. The program's success and sustainability continues to be driven by Ms. Bowen's vision, persuasion, persistence, and most of all, leadership.

STEP THREE. TRAINING MANAGERS AND TELEWORKERS

When the telework program is initiated, both managers and employees – including office workers and teleworkers – need to be "on the same page." And naturally everyone will have a lot of questions. Bring them all together whether or not they plan to telework because it is important that everyone hears the same message, right from the start.

Remember

A Program That Works For Everyone

Make sure from the beginning that everyone is aware that teleworking has little if any impact the organization's business focus. Stress that teleworking is not a perk or an entitlement but a way for employees to be more productive and performance-oriented, while providing opportunities for better work/life balance. Everyone needs to understand their job responsibilities; for instance, deadlines remain the same even if you are working remotely.

Must Do

Establish ground rules and procedures that ensure productivity and collaboration. Discuss your communication needs and clarify procedures, such as how to know if it's someone's telework day. Take time to walk through the agency's telework policy and guidelines, and review eligibility criteria.

Spend time talking about what can go wrong. Telework introduces new ways of working together; encourage your employees to think about potential problems before they happen.

Tips

Complete a Telework Agreement for Each Telework Employee

Most organizations have a telework agreement. As a manager, you'll find the agreement to be an invaluable tool for guiding your discussion with the prospective teleworker, and for recording his or her commitments. Ideally, the manager and the employee will first have a thorough conversation about the employee's job responsibilities, including how to perform well as a teleworker.

Rather than being a performance plan, the agreement documents the specific arrangements and agreements between the manager and the employee. It will include things, such as how many days per week or pay period the employee can telework, their core hours, and clarification on what the agency will pay for (such as a laptop, business phone, Internet service, etc.), versus what the employee must provide. Both parties, supervisor and employee, must sign the agreement.

Communicate Regularly for Productivity and Performance

! Must Do Measuring your employees' performance isn't about seeing them busily active – it's about seeing real results. Whether or not your employees are teleworkers, they should be clear on their job responsibilities and deliverables. Teleworkers must plan their work carefully to ensure they are productive both at home and in the office. Be very specific about how you want to be kept informed about their accomplishments. Talk with your teleworkers about meaningful measures of productivity, and the results you expect to see in terms of productivity, quality, and timeliness. Spend plenty of time on key measures of performance, such as effectiveness in communications, planning, and collaboration.

Rather than waiting for a formal evaluation period, provide consistent and frequent communication and feedback. Feedback is important for your employees so that they can improve and/or know that they are on track. And even though there's a physical distance between you and your telework employees, you can provide routine feedback through emails, phone calls or faxes. Use face-to-face meetings for significant feedback, as well as relationship- and trust-building.

Consider Tools for Efficiency and Collaboration

Tips Investigate hardware and software solutions that might help your team communicate and work together effectively when in different locations. Bring the team together to assess the nature of their work, and the kind of communication tools they need. Are group sessions important for exploring ideas? Do you need information-sharing tools, or project-management interaction? Depending on your needs, these solutions could range from larger-scale tools, such as installing videoconferencing facilities, to simpler things, such as setting up a team Website or project message center for general information sharing. You may want to add a chat room or discussion area to your Website, as well. Be sure to include your IT experts as you strategize solutions, so they can help with integration and security. Arrange for training, if necessary, to ensure your team's ability to use any new tools you introduce.

Maintain Harmony in the Office

As a manager, do your best to maintain a balance between the needs of your telework and office staff. Make sure everyone receives fair, equitable treatment regardless of where they work. Avoid singling out one group over the other.

Tips **Here are some suggestions for achieving balance:**
- ☐ Keep everyone in the loop through email messages and a computer calendar system.
- ☐ Encourage healthy partnerships among all team members; consider opportunities for mentoring and cross-training, and be sure to reward good examples of collaboration.
- ☐ Hold meaningful meetings and use business reasons to determine when teleworkers should be physically present.
- ☐ Clearly communicate rules for things that apply equally to teleworkers and nonteleworkers, such as vacation, sick leave, and overtime.

Step Three. Training Managers and Teleworkers

- ☐ Keep communication open and provide guidance at all times. Be ready to react quickly and appropriately if there's ever a breakdown; for example if the in-office staff forgets to include teleworkers in an important meeting.
- ☐ Remember your teleworkers' professional development.

Many potential teleworkers have real concerns that they'll miss important opportunities if they're not in the office every day. Others may get so comfortable working without distractions at home, that they forget the importance of team participation. It's the manager's job to support the professional development of every employee. You may need to remind your teleworkers to pay more attention to their own career development when they work remotely. Encourage them to use their in-office days for face-to-face meetings, networking, and relationship building. Challenge your employees to go after assignments and opportunities that showcase their strengths. Reward strong collaboration among all your employees, so they see that team synergy is critical even when working in different locations. And always be an advocate for your teleworkers. When you're focused on the work they're producing, rather than where they're doing it, you can speak up on behalf of their successes.

Acknowledge Your Employees' Achievements

If telework is having a positive impact on your employees, the team, and the work you all do, let people know! Connect your appreciation to results: individual accountability, productivity, performance, and collaboration. Help employees work through change, and acknowledge their successes. Share the positive impact of your telework program with peers and senior management, too – make sure you present your successes in terms of how they specifically benefit the organization.

Training Managers

Assess Your Management Style!

This self-assessment can assist you in identifying your potential levels of success in managing in a virtual environment. Rather than being a "pass" or "fail" test, this self-assessment is designed to provide insight into the characteristics needed to successfully manage teleworkers.

Rank yourself on each of the following elements by putting an "X" on the appropriate line. A rating of 5 is considered excellent or high, while a rating of 1 is considered low, with 2s and 3s meaning some work needs to be done. Be honest, since this can help you assess areas of need (rather than indicating failure).

MANAGEMENT CHARACTERISTICS	5	4	3	2	1
Manages by objectives and results	__	__	__	__	__
Comfortable with remote supervision	__	__	__	__	__
Ability to be flexible with work schedules	__	__	__	__	__

MANAGEMENT CHARACTERISTICS	5	4	3	2	1
Communicates regularly with subordinates	—	—	—	—	—
Coaches/counsels employees regularly	—	—	—	—	—
Trust level with subordinates	—	—	—	—	—
Promotes employee empowerment	—	—	—	—	—
Receptive to new ideas	—	—	—	—	—

Now that you have identified characteristics needing improvement, determine what you need to do to improve your "rating." This book contains many suggestions to help change low indicators to high. In some cases, you need only to experience managing remotely and the best advice is to "just do it."

Managerial Style and Expectations

The following are some typical issues for managers of telecommuters, and suggested approaches for dealing with them.

The Need for a Flexible Approach

Despite thorough preparation and planning, most telecommuters and their managers will need to do some fine-tuning to the work arrangements once the employee begins telecommuting. For example, after being in the program for a while, some telecommuters may find they would prefer more or less time at the alternate worksite. Managers may determine that a different work schedule would be more suitable for the organization. Managers should maintain flexibility on program parameters, especially at the beginning when both the manager and the employee are likely to encounter adjustment issues.

Clear Assignments and Expectations

Regardless of the work arrangement, ensure that work assignments and performance expectations are clear and mutually understood by the manager and the employee. With telecommuting, however, the importance of clear communications and a mutual understanding of expectations is heightened.

Because you are managing by results, the employee must be made aware of what is expected of him/her in terms of work assignments and performance. Don't assume that the employee knows what you want without your discussing it first. The manager should also set benchmarks for teleworkers as to the manner and frequency of communication and/or reporting needed. For example, the manager and the employee should discuss how often and when the employee is expected to check e-mails and voice mails.

Step Three. Training Managers and Teleworkers

Also:

☐ Describe the work assignments and objectives in clear and concise terms.

☐ Ensure that assignments are clearly understood by asking probing questions.

☐ Clearly state the date the assignment and/or its parts are due.

☐ Encourage the employee to ask questions, and then answer them honestly.

Using Progress Reporting

With many jobs, work output is not necessarily a concrete and directly measurable product. The work may be part of a long-term project, involving developing relationships, reading, reviewing, studying, conceptualizing, etc. None of these results are tangible.

Tips

Even with tangible results, the manager may not have a basis, or simply not know, how to determine quality or appropriate time requirements for the completion of a given assignment. For these situations, a progress report can be used to measure output. Such reports inform the manager and serve as a useful mechanism during the initial adjustment period. Finally, adequate progress reporting can ascertain what is involved in various assignments and how long they take to complete.

Another way to manage the work of your offsite employee is to develop a formal plan for long-term assignments that involve many facets. A well-executed plan sets the stage for performance expectations and enables the manager and the employee to jointly prepare and commit to delivering a specific work product in a specific period of time.

Staying Connected

Managers should make the extra effort to help telecommuters stay connected to the organization.

Must Do

When possible, managers should:

☐ Ensure that telecommuters receive all office communications in a timely fashion.

☐ Schedule meetings on days the telecommuter is in the office or set up meetings to include the telecommuter via audio or video conference or other electronic means.

☐ Ensure the telecommuter remains aware of and involved in official events, decision making discussions, and group planning sessions.

☐ Have an office discussion including the telecommuters and coworkers on ways to maintain communications and preserve teamwork.

www.GovernmentTrainingInc.com

Addressing Fairness/Morale Problems

No No — An unfortunate issue that has clouded telework is fairness in assignments and promotions. Favoritism and unfairness in assignments and promotions can occur in any organization; with telecommuting, however, this issue sometimes gets more attention. In many cases, telecommuters will miss choice assignments or opportunities for promotions because they are not around to gain as much favor or have as much face-to-face contact. In some cases, this unfairness is unintentional; more of a simple oversight by the manager (out of sight, out of mind). To avoid or assuage concern over this problem, managers should sensitize themselves to this issue and, most importantly, have a frank and open discussion with telecommuters. Not only should managers reassure teleworkers that they will avoid such behavior, but they should encourage the employees to come forward with any questions or issues.

Managers have expressed concern about possible morale problems and/or grievances from employees not allowed to participate in telecommuting. Some managers may be inclined to rule out participation for everyone because of such concerns or preconceived notions. One approach for reducing the possibility of morale problems and/or grievances is to establish a clear set of criteria for employee selection into the program (see page 51 for information on selection criteria) and then publicize these criteria. This not only gives employees a clear awareness of the selection criteria but also provides non-participants an incentive to improve performance.

Remember — The manager and the employee should have a positive working relationship before beginning telecommuting. If you, as the manager, identify areas of nonperformance, lack of trust, or dependency on direct supervision, wait until these problems are resolved before allowing the employee to telecommute. Managers should provide the true reasons for denying an employee's request for telecommuting. In addition, the necessary steps to improve the employee's performance should be identified along with the time frame for reevaluation of the request. When the criteria are met, the employee should be allowed to begin telecommuting. This positive approach puts the responsibility for showing suitability for telecommuting on the worker rather than the manager.

A common "what if" expressed by managers is when two employees apply for telecommuting and both have acceptable performance appraisals, but the manager is uncomfortable with a subjective quality of one of the employees e.g. the employee does his/her job well but needs a great deal of supervision. In this instance, the manager can allow the independent employee to participate and use this as an opportunity to work with the other employee to change. By using telecommuting as a motivator or incentive, the less independent employee is offered a chance to change his/her work habits for the better. The problem may be remedied after a period of time and the initial request reconsidered. Another approach is to allow the employee to telecommute on a provisional basis. The latter includes a written statement that the employee will be removed from the program unless specific goals/benchmarks are accomplished within a mutually agreed upon time frame.

Step Three. Training Managers and Teleworkers

Feedback For Telecommuters

When giving feedback:

- ☐ Make feedback a regular scheduled component of your relationship with the telecommuting employee.
- ☐ If there is a reason for unscheduled feedback try to provide that feedback immediately after the need is recognized.
- ☐ Give the feedback in private and make sure you have time to discuss it with the employee.
- ☐ Balance positive and negative feedback.
- ☐ Discuss the duties of the job, not the worker. Also ensure that you have firsthand knowledge of, or written information about, any action you mention.
- ☐ Be honest, direct, and specific about your expectations. For example, if you schedule a meeting on a telecommuting day, let the telecommuter know whether they should attend in person, by telephone, or not at all. As with any employee, avoid making the telecommuter guess or assume that they know what you want.
- ☐ Respect the telecommuting arrangement; it is a contract between you and the employee. Honor every aspect and make sure it is implemented properly.
- ☐ Give oral and written signals to all staff members that you support telecommuting and take it seriously. Make sure that all employees know you expect them to do the same and make sure everyone avoids characterizing telecommuting as "goofing off" or "getting away with not working".

The Magnificent Seven Telework Tips for Managers – How to Ensure Employees are Comfortable with Telework

Tips

1. **If the Shoe Fits.** Not all positions are telework friendly and not all employees are a fit for telework. Research job requirements and past job performance to determine telework eligibility. Revisit employees' eligibility options periodically – there is a pressing requirement to standardize eligibility assessment for employees across agencies.

2. **Education Is Imperative.** Focus on training. Make sure your employees are comfortable in their telework situation. They must be culturally and technologically ready for telework.

3. **Slow and Steady.** Offer a phased approach. Implement a program so that workers can start by teleworking one or two days a week. This ensures that teleworkers are comfortable in the transition. Also new employees may need to phase into full-time telework.

4. **Home Away from Home.** If feasible, offer an option to work at a telework center. A telework center provides opportunities to network with peers, eliminates social isolation, and adheres to agency security requirements.

www.GovernmentTrainingInc.com

Handbook for Managing Teleworkers – Toolkit

5. **Get the Full Picture.** Research available technology to enhance the depth and quality of interactions with remote coworkers. Video communication technology has become increasingly more affordable and easy to implement. Video communication takes teleworking to a higher-valued level – beyond telephone and email telework models.

6. **Safe and Secure.** Ensure that employees follow security protocols. Talk with your employees to make sure they are aware of and have the resources to follow agency security guidelines.

7. **Different Strokes for Different Folks.** Each teleworker works differently. Periodically check in with your employees to see how things are going. Discuss pain points and strategize on solutions.

Adapted from: Telework Exchange

USA Learning For Managers

Tips

USA Learning, The Official Learning and Development Site for the Federal government has added a new course to its free catalogue, Telework 101 for Managers: Making Telework Work for You. Telework can help managers attract and retain the best qualified employees, provide them with uninterrupted blocks of time to work on key projects, and give their organization a way of functioning more effectively during crisis situations and other business interruptions. The course introduces managers to basic telework concepts. It walks managers through the process of developing a program, selecting employees for telework, and managing effectively in a telework environment and helps them structure their telework program in a way that avoids common pitfalls. Telework training for managers is available through USA Learning, go to *http://www.usalearning.gov/USALearning/*.

Telework Pitfalls

New telecommuter and their supervisors may encounter common pitfalls and traps that have already been identified. Fortunately, ways to avoid these situations have also been developed. Much of the training for employees and their supervisors addresses how to get started correctly and how to deal with problem situations as they arise.

However, follows are some of the more common pitfalls and traps.

☐ Managers routinely plan important meetings during scheduled work at home days.

- Alternative: Negotiate a telework schedule that is more compatible with office needs or, whenever possible, set up a conference call.

☐ Coworkers don't know when the teleworker will be in the office. There is a general sense that the teleworker is "never around."

- Alternative: Post a schedule when each employee is in the office and when they are out (either teleworking or on approved leave).

☐ Managers and teleworkers do not have a clear understanding of work expectations.

- Alternative: Define work expectations in advance to avoid misunderstanding and periodically review the agreement to ensure its adequacy.

Step Three. Training Managers and Teleworkers

- ☐ Coworkers are not able to contact the teleworker (and are sometimes actively discouraged). Clerical staff are unclear on how or when to contact the teleworker. There is a reluctance to call teleworkers at home on their telework days.
    - ■ Alternative: Provide staff with the teleworker's remote office phone number. Encourage staff to call them on telework days. Supervisors should set an example by calling teleworkers on their home work days and insisting that others continue to transact business with employees at home.
- ☐ Teleworkers are reluctant to leave the phone on their telework days, even to use the restroom or take a break, because someone who called might think they are not working.
    - ■ Alternative: Use an answering machine to take messages during absences. The teleworker should follow-up with caller immediately upon their return.
- ☐ Teleworkers run into technical problems with their computers and no one is available to assist them.
    - ■ Alternative: Establish procedures for call-in trouble shooting.
- ☐ Telework is joked about as "goofing off". Telework days are referred to by coworkers as days off.
    - ■ Alternative: Provide information on the benefits of telework to staff members. Make visible the work products that the teleworker produces while working at home.
- ☐ Teleworker feels a sense of isolation and loss of interaction with coworkers.
    - ■ Alternative: Encourage active communication via email and telephone between telecommuters and in-office staff. Consider use of a telework center or increase the number of days in the primary office.
- ☐ Teleworker's home/work boundaries are blurred.
    - ■ Alternative: Keep the home office separate from the living area by placing it in a separate room as far removed from the living areas as possible. Keep a definite schedule of work time and personal time and adhere to it.
- ☐ The organization incurs additional expenses associated with the provision of equipment and services such as telephone charges for computer connections and long-distance call.
    - ■ Alternative: Weigh additional costs against current and projected organizational needs. Factor in office space savings, potential recruitment savings, savings in training funds, and other "bottom line" savings to the organization.

Training Teleworkers

The employees you select to telework should be self-disciplined, independent, and results-driven. Employees who perform well onsite will most likely perform well no matter where they work. Before implementing your program, however, employees need to be trained. Be aware of:

- ☐ Your agency's telework goals
- ☐ What makes a successful teleworker
- ☐ Suitable teleworker characteristics
- ☐ Red flags
- ☐ Team success factors
- ☐ Leveraging the technology
- ☐ Maximizing virtual meetings
- ☐ Facing the challenges

Checklist

Training should include:
- ☐ Equipment and software
- ☐ Organizational and employee equipment liability
- ☐ Information security

Working at home challenges
- ☐ How to "Get a buddy" – someone you can go to for advice
- ☐ Creating and organizing your workspace
- ☐ Staying in touch with the office
- ☐ Obtaining supervisor feedback

Training employees before the program is only the beginning. Ongoing training should be utilized as the program grows. Teleworkers will need to be able to:

- ☐ Build trust with supervisors
- ☐ Avoid misconceptions by coworkers
- ☐ Create a seamless environment for customers
- ☐ Plan for a productive day
- ☐ Avoid creating additional work for others
- ☐ Avoid overworking (know when and how to end the workday)
- ☐ Avoid procrastination
- ☐ Avoid potential household distractions

Step Three. Training Managers and Teleworkers

Identify Your Training Audiences

Training is beneficial for anyone who interacts with a teleworker, whether they are based in the office or not. Everyone should know the eligibility factors, processes, policy, and guidelines to help manage program expectations. Training everyone will ensure a smoother launch. Consider including the following in your telework training:

- ☐ Teleworkers
- ☐ Any onsite employees who interact with teleworkers. These employees will learn effective ways of communicating with those offsite
- ☐ Members of your IT or technology division. Most likely, your teleworkers will rely on technology and should be trained by IT staff on all applicable policies, as well as how to access servers, email, and so on.

> **Tips**
> Hold pre-telework training sessions for all employees. These sessions will help ensure success. By training more than just your teleworkers, you can help integrate new business practices across the whole team. Follows are some suggestions for pre-telework training topics for employees. The format, structure, number, and type of sessions is up to you, as these are best determined by your agency's size, culture, and how you typically handle agency training.

Discuss your organization's goals for establishing a telework program:

- ☐ Enable work anytime, anywhere
- ☐ Reduce real estate/costs
- ☐ Enhance recruiting, and retain valuable employees
- ☐ Business continuity
- ☐ Expand options for Americans With Disabilities ACT (ADA) accommodation
- ☐ Increase productivity and work quality
- ☐ Increase collaboration
- ☐ Encourage management by results
- ☐ Contribute to improved traffic congestion/air quality

Discuss items in place to help ensure the telework program success:

- ☐ Policy and program well-suited to the organization
- ☐ Business focus: goals and metrics
- ☐ Administrative infrastructure
- ☐ The right technology
- ☐ Optimal support system

Handbook for Managing Teleworkers – Toolkit

- ☐ Communications strategy
- ☐ Training for stakeholders

Discuss factors that will help ensure the success of your teleworking teams:

- ☐ Communication
- ☐ Best practices
- ☐ Meetings: how, when, who
- ☐ Face time
- ☐ Sharing data, experiences
- ☐ Honesty
- ☐ Tracking and reporting
- ☐ Set goals
- ☐ Measure success
- ☐ Refine
- ☐ Celebrate

Discuss characteristics of successful teleworkers:

- ☐ Self-motivated, self-managing
- ☐ Results-oriented
- ☐ Conscientious, organized
- ☐ Independent worker
- ☐ Flexible
- ☐ Understands job requirements
- ☐ Understands organizational policies and procedures
- ☐ Communicates well with colleagues and clients
- ☐ Handles change well

Discuss how teleworkers will communicate with their managers and coworkers:

- ☐ Leverage the technology
- ☐ Reach out and touch: phone, voicemail, cell phones, speakerphones
- ☐ Make email an information tool, not a communication tool
- ☐ Share space on the Intra- or Internet
- ☐ Maximize videoconferencing
- ☐ Try collaboration software tools

Step Three. Training Managers and Teleworkers

- ☐ Maximize virtual meetings
- ☐ Prepare and distribute agenda
- ☐ Agree upon meeting outcomes
- ☐ Propose procedures (e.g., polling, voting) and signals
- ☐ Decide on tone: formal or informal
- ☐ Agree on leadership
- ☐ Agree on ground rules
- ☐ Confirm outcomes, next steps, responsibilities
- ☐ De-brief before closing

Discuss employee concerns and other potential issues your group can foresee, and brainstorm solutions:

- ☐ What if I'm the only one in the office?
- ☐ What if more work falls on me?
- ☐ What if my backup isn't performing the way I need them to?
- ☐ What if I don't like teleworking?
- ☐ What if someone on the team isn't pulling their weight?

Success Stories

American Speech-Language-Hearing Association

The American Speech-Language-Hearing Association (ASHA) is the professional, scientific and credentialing association for more than 127,000 members and affiliates who are speech-language pathologists, audiologists, and speech, language, and hearing scientists in the United States and internationally.

The mission of the American Speech- Language-Hearing Association is to empower and support speech-language pathologists, audiologists, and speech, language, and hearing scientists by: advocating on behalf of persons with communication and related disorders, advancing communication science, and promoting effective human communication. ASHA began planning their telework program in August of 1994 and conducted their first pilot in January of 1995. The timeline and components of ASHA's telework program are as follows:

- ☐ August – October 1994 – form staff team and create plan
- ☐ November 1994 – present to executive team and staff
- ☐ December 1994 – training, focus groups and data gathering
- ☐ January – March 1995 – conduct pilot program

☐ March 1995 – focus groups, data gathering and presentation to executive team 20 percent of the staff currently telecommute on a regular basis, but many others flexplace, or work from home in the evenings and over the weekend.

The Telework Experience

ASHA distinguished two types of telework – flexplace and telecommuting. Flexplace is a cooperative arrangement that allows an employee to work on a specific project from home or other work site outside the National Office on an occasional basis. Flexplace is a less formal arrangement than Telecommuting. All staff are eligible to participate, subject to their coach's approval. If you are using Flexplace, ASHA's expectations are that:

☐ You need to work on a particular project or tasks

☐ You want/need seclusion and may request not to be interrupted. (These requests must be pre-planned and discussed ahead of time with your coach.)

☐ Someone should be able to contact you in the event of an urgent/critical need.

☐ Flexplace is not to be used in lieu of childcare.

☐ Opportunities are granted at the discretion of the coach.

☐ Your coach may request that you adjust your plans if issues should arise related to providing adequate coverage in your unit.

☐ Coaches should monitor productivity and availability and address issues that do not further the goals of the team.

Telecommuting is a cooperative work arrangement whereby an employee works from home or other work site outside the National Office for a regularly scheduled portion of each week. An eligible employee can telecommute up to 60 percent of the time he/she is scheduled to work (for fulltime employees up to 3 days a week) with the consent of the coach and appropriate Facilitating Team member. It is expected that the employee will be as accessible as his/her onsite counterparts. The employee communicates with other employees in the National Office, members, customers, and other business contacts via computer, telephone, fax, or other equipment.

Eligible employees for telecommuting:

☐ Can be either full-time or part-time/exempt or nonexempt

☐ Must have been employed by ASHA for at least 1 year

☐ Must have worked in present position for at least 6 months

☐ Must have "meets expectations" on most recent performance management review

☐ Must have a clearly defined work space

☐ Must have access to needed references, computer equipment, and telephone systems

Step Three. Training Managers and Teleworkers

If you are telecommuting, ASHA expects that:

- ☐ You will be as available to others in the office as you would be if you were here in the office. You have simply changed your work location.
- ☐ Your availability should be obvious, either via a note on your computer monitor, doorway, door, or some other obvious place, so individuals looking for you, get an idea of where/how to find you.
- ☐ You should be available for meetings (by telephone).
- ☐ You will provide contact information (a phone number) so that someone in the office can contact you, if necessary. (Note: Please do not post your home telephone or personal cell phone numbers…either provide that information to others in your team or to some other staff person(s) with whom you are working, and post a note to let others know who has your contact information.)
- ☐ Your voicemail message should indicate that you are working away from the office and provide contact information for the individual(s) who knows how to reach you. Also, provide an indication of how often you will be checking your voicemail, and make sure you check your voicemail regularly.
- ☐ Your telecommuting days/times should be regular.
- ☐ Telecommuting is not to be used in lieu of childcare.
- ☐ Opportunities are granted at the discretion of the coach.
- ☐ Your coach may request that you adjust your plans if issues should arise related to providing adequate coverage in your unit.
- ☐ Coaches should monitor productivity and availability and address issues that do not further the goals of the team. The theory is that teleworkers have fewer distractions when working remotely. For teleworking employees, relief from worsening congestion and the increasing costs of commuting have provided increased employee morale and satisfaction.

Challenges & Investment

As telework is considered a natural fit for the culture of ASHA, there was very little management resistance to the program. In most cases, teleworkers are responsible for acquiring all of the hardware and software necessary for their participation. However, in accordance with their goal to keep staff technologically up to date, ASHA offers a benefit that allows employees to purchase computers and related equipment/software, etc. through a payroll deduction plan for their use at home. Employees choose their purchases, have ASHA produce a check for payment, and then pay back ASHA over the course of 26 pay periods or less.

Program Outlook

A number of organizational conditions are changing at ASHA that make this an ideal time to reassess their needs and how well they are being met. ASHA will be moving to a new building requiring a longer commute for some staff. In addition, ASHA will no longer be assessable by Metro Rail.

Commuting time in the area is also on the rise due to traffic congestion. The cost of gas is increasing resulting in increased commuting costs. Aspects of ASHA's disaster recovery plan rely on staff being able or perform crucial portions of their jobs from home.

A Remote Access Team was established in 2007. The team has conducted a thorough survey of the staff to find out what teleworkers need to be able to perform their key responsibilities from home for their position. ASHA is assessing which of these things are currently available and rank what else might be needed in the order of importance/greatest impact. Modifications to the program will be made according to the impact of each change and investment in time and resources.

Success Tips

- ☐ The early development of a cross functional team responsible for designing and piloting the telework program was critical to its success.
- ☐ Formalizing participation requirements and expectations was important in focusing the program on the most suitable employees and job tasks.
- ☐ Not excluding any positions by team or title helped to place the focus on meeting ASHA's business needs.
- ☐ Collecting data on the success and any issues with the program paid off by giving the team objective data on which to base the decision to continue the program and what modifications needed to be made.

National Institutes of Health

The National Institutes of Health (NIH), a part of the U.S. Department of Health and Human Services, is the primary Federal agency that conducts and supports biomedical and behavioral research to improve people's health and save lives. Flexibility is a practiced principle at NIH, necessary to accomplish research and research support at multiple locations. Employees here must have an adaptable work environment to effectively support mission-related needs.

Telework initially began at NIH as a flexible workplace arrangement benefit that was primarily used by employees as an accommodation to meet short-term medical needs. A successful one year pilot in 2001 to examine its benefits, costs, and impacts on employees, management, and the organization resulted in an expansion of the early initiative to a fully implemented program. Participation has grown steadily as a result of several things, recruiting and retention efforts, a new leadership team, and continuity of operations planning.

Step Three. Training Managers and Teleworkers

"Telework has proven itself to be a win-win strategy for increasing both employee satisfaction and productivity", says Christine Major, Director of the NIH Office of Human Resources. "Ours is an evolving model, with staff in a growing number of positions able to work effectively wherever they are and enjoy the benefits of telework." The goal of the program is to help staff be successful and effective with teleworking so that in the long term, they contribute to a business solution trusted by managers, peers and the organization – a responsibility not taken lightly by NIH.

The Telework Experience

The telework experience is critical to NIH's human resources mission, something the HR leaders at NIH are very passionate about. According to Philip Lenowitz, the Deputy Director of NIH's Office of Human Resources (OHR), "Our mission – the whole reason we're here – has always been to recruit and retain the best employees for NIH". From the employee's perspective, teleworking provides individuals the opportunity to support NIH's mission from a comfortable atmosphere, while avoiding the traditional daily work related stressors.

Well-intentioned interruptions at work, the daily commute, and even technology overload are all work-related factors that can lead to stress. There are many more benefits to teleworking other than alleviating the stress factor though. Decreasing traffic and helping the environment, optimizing the use of technology, accommodating people with disabilities, and reducing absenteeism by allowing greater flexibility are a few more of the benefits. NIH leadership and management believe the resulting improvement in the quality of life for NIH employees can lead to improvements in morale, productivity, and retention.

An extensive telework policy has been put in place for NIH employees. Both full-time and part-time employees are eligible to apply who do not have any evidence of misconduct in their records and are not required to complete all their work onsite. In addition, the employee must be able to complete the majority of their work from a remote location that does not require the resources that working onsite provides (ex. constant face-to-face communication with team members, constant meetings with personnel outside their teams, usage of agency resources that can only be found onsite, etc.).

NIH provides very specific guidelines for establishing, monitoring, and measuring the effectiveness of telework arrangements. In order to be approved to telework, the employee has to develop a proposal via an agreement form and then discuss it with their supervisor. Among other things, the employee agrees to work diligently from a remote location in a space that they have dedicated solely for performing their work offsite. Resources are made available to both those navigating and managing the process, for example, in-depth training courses for managers and potential teleworkers covering everything from performance management to setting up and actually working in a virtual environment.

Personalized guidance from knowledgeable internal experts is available for completing or reviewing proposals. As supervisors analyze proposals and monitor arrangements, they look at tasks, the effect on work groups, and office needs to reduce the potential for negative impacts to either individual or group performance. The IT and HR organizations are very proactive parts of the program, providing support to make user experiences, whether managerial or individual, as smooth as possible.

Challenges & Investment

In spite of the challenges that come with implementing telework, NIH has been able to adopt the teleworking concept for a wide variety positions. While many positions at NIH are conducive to teleworking, internal organizations are encouraged to look at further utilizing the opportunities it presents, e.g., the technology. NIH does research on an extremely wide variety of health matters.

The medical research field is a more difficult scenario for teleworking because an employee cannot take an entire research laboratory home with them. They often can, however, telework doing some tasks such as transcribing findings into reports, journals, etc...

Out of necessity then, teleworking is very customizable at NIH, due in part to the nature of the work and the support needs that may be involved, e.g., with regard to types of arrangements or equipment to be provided. Employees with certain responsibilities who telework regularly may be issued Blackberries and laptops or, in cases where a Blackberry isn't appropriate or available, wireless broadband cards might be used to allow employees to connect into NIH wherever they get a cell phone connection.

Program Outlook

The teleworking program at NIH has a very positive outlook. It has the support of the top NIH leadership, all of whom encourage staff to take part if the nature of their work is a good fit for it. As with the investment of resources, the NIH telework policy, telework training, and outreach to managers and staff are all works in progress.

Step Three. Training Managers and Teleworkers

Success Tips

- ☐ Collaborate with others. If you have a question or want to see how teleworking is being addressed in organizations similar to yours, don't hesitate to ask.
- ☐ Employee feedback is one of the most valuable tools to a newly implemented program. Utilize the employees that have been a part of the program and work with them to find out what works, what needs improvement, and for promoting the program.
- ☐ With any new initiative, always be open to learning new technologies. Technology advancements, especially those within communications, are always expanding and can be utilized to help further your program.
- ☐ Encourage telework solutions that seek to provide efficient use of resources. Telework is not an all-or nothing proposition, but rather is intended to promote flexibility, so being flexible with how it's implemented is important.

Helpful Resources

The general atmosphere and culture of NIH greatly contributed to the success of telework in the Agency.

When your mission involves finding the next medical breakthrough, implementing a flexibility initiative like telework is more readily accepted.

NIH has established a Telework Focus Group to further expand telework.

The agency consulted other government agencies, such as the Office of Personnel Management, General Services Administration, National Science Foundation, and the U.S. Department of Agriculture, among others, on teleworking issues.

Step Four. Motivation: Developing and Building Trust and Mentoring

Motivation is especially important in telecommuting, because there is so much physical distance between you and your workers. This is true of every job, from call center employees to high-level executives who manage dozens of virtual teams around the globe. If you believe your employees are doing their job properly -- and if they think you are providing competent and fair guidance and direction – then things will move along smoothly most of the time.

Remember

The Importance Of Trust

An easy way of establishing trust is to work with a known quantity; that is, employees who have been with your organization for a while and/or with whom you have a rapport or workers experienced in their field who can provide references or have a proven track record. However, circumstances may be such that you may have to go "outside" and hire someone completely new. In that case, networking can come in handy; for example, a colleague or peer can recommend a worker within the organization or field of endeavor. Local colleges or trade schools can be especially helpful in supplying recent graduates or leads, especially if you are looking for teleworkers in a geographic area that you're unfamiliar with. Likewise, personnel or temp agencies can be a source of reliable clerical or customer support referrals although of course, most charge for this service.

Many times your instincts will tell you who to trust. Does the worker appear to learn quickly and display enthusiasm during training and in your various communications? Does she express an interest in the agency and its goals along with a willingness to learn new things? Does she make that extra effort to satisfy the customer or end user rather than shrugging and saying, "It's not my job?" Is she willing to participate in meetings, either on-site or remotely, to get to know members of the team and share information? During training, if a new hire seems unresponsive or disengaged, you might want to watch them closely to make sure they're actually capable (and willing) to do the job.

Tips

Most of us have an internal trip wire that goes off whenever we encounter someone who may not be trustworthy. Often this is triggered by such cues as a lack of eye contact or a bored tone of voice or just a sense that their personality might not mesh well with the team. Because you are not physically seeing the individual or probably even speaking with him daily, telecommuting adds an extra layer of distance, so it's especially important to have a positive "gut feeling" about this person, whether you're meeting him face-to-face or over the phone. When it comes to establishing trust there's no substitute for either type of contact during the interview process.

One the person is hired, you can take specific steps to foster trust among team members.

- ☐ **Open and honest communication.** The only way employees will know what you're thinking is if you tell them directly.
- ☐ **Give trust to get trust.** This can seem like a bit of a risk, especially if you've been accustomed to managing workers in an office. But "leading by example" sets the stage for an atmosphere of mutual trust and encourages others to trust you back (Remember "Innocent until proven guilty"?). Especially at the beginning, if you communicate mistrust, then it may very well condemn the team – and the project -- to an atmosphere of negativity and suspicion.
- ☐ **Honesty is always the best policy.** Although they are physically removed from the rumor mill and corporate politics, telecommuters hear things as well. However, if you are upfront with them about the good, bad, and the not-so-certain, they will feel they can come to you with questions and concerns. If you are bound by confidentiality in not revealing specific information -- say, a corporate takeover and/or layoffs are imminent but nothing is confirmed -- then tell them you do not yet have concrete answers (the truth) and you will get back with them as soon as you know something for sure.

Even if you make a mistake or don't know something, it's better to admit that than try to cover it up or "bs" your way out of it. Most people have can sense when they are being stonewalled and nothing undermines trust faster than that.

- ☐ **Establish a core set of business ethics.** These basic standards of honesty, decency, and behavior should be set forth as part of the agency culture and work plan and agreed upon, understood, and internalized by all team members. Ethics are the glue which hold teams together, and are especially important to those separated by time and space, allowing them operate under common beliefs and the same principles.
- ☐ **Follow through.** If you say you're going to do something, do it, and do it out loud. Team members should know that for better or worse, if you say it, you'll git 'r' done. Don't be like the joke, "Do what I say, not what I do."
- ☐ **Be consistent.** This works well both in sports and in business. If your team members know you're going to react logically and fairly to mistakes and problems, then they will more willing to approach you. Unpredictable reactions, however, elicit the opposite response and can set the stage for cover-ups and misunderstandings.

Step Four. Motivation: Developing and Building Trust and Mentoring

- ☐ **Be responsive and available.** This can be tricky, given variances in time zones and work hours. No matter how you implement the system of communication, employees need to know you'll get back to them within a certain time.

- ☐ **Ask questions.** Diverse teams may use different cultural slang and points of reference. Be sensitive to these, and ask for clarification to avoid confusion and misunderstandings. This is true whether you're dealing with face-to-face meetings, teleconferences, or written communications, such as e-mails.

- ☐ **Be trustworthy.** Sometimes employees will come to you with personal information or express concerns about work-related matters or even personality conflicts. As with office workers, it's important to keep this confidential, even if they are scattered around the globe. The best way to keep a secret is to keep it to yourself.

- ☐ **Be generous with praise and include everyone.** Professional development classes, incentives, and social gatherings, even if they are infrequent and informal, help build and cement relationships. Take the time to get to know your team members, and ask about their families and hobbies (making sure not get too personal of course, or break any confidences). For example, workers "bond" during ARO virtual training seminars by sharing their hobbies and interests with the group.

Trust Quiz

True or False....

☐ As a manager/leader, "I know" that I get full and open communication with my employees.

☐ I openly, honestly and fully communicate with my boss.

☐ Our agency receives a large number of creative cost saving ideas from our employees.

☐ Our management meetings are open to all employees.

☐ I personally have a high/low trust level of others

☐ I can be trusted to keep my word with others.

Take a moment to look over the questions in the quiz. Notice your responses....are your answers a symptom of individual and/ or organizational lack of trust? Or have you helped to create an environment that will help you keep your valued staff and team members as we move into an uncertain business future? What would it take to re-instill a culture of openness and trust?

Source: *Mastermind Learning Network Newsletter, Oct. 2001, http://www.jackwolflearning.com/newsletter/pdf.asp?ID=52*

How to Build Trust

The relationship between an employee and an employer is already based on trust and many factors influence the level of trust involved. External factors, training and skills, and past experiences can all complicate the issue. The three central factors are:

- ☐ A solid personal relationship
- ☐ Knowing that the person has the necessary qualifications and skills
- ☐ Being able to monitor performance.

Strong relationships are built on three things: time, knowledge, and contact, in various combinations. The longer you have known someone the more likely you are to trust them. The more you know about how they react, and their personal lives, such as hobbies and sports, the higher your trust will become. Effective personal contact will reinforce your trust even more.

Managers can develop stronger relationships in many relatively simple and obvious ways:

- ☐ Don't rush it. Strong relationships take time to develop.
- ☐ Honesty is important. Saying what you mean (tactfully) and meaning what you say ensures that employees will come to respect you. And it is impossible to build a meaningful relationship with someone you lie to—even if they don't know you're lying.
- ☐ Fairness is important. Treating all staff the same is critical to the development of good working relationships.
- ☐ Involve all employees in decision making. This will help them feel that their input is valued and they will trust you.
- ☐ Try not to talk about work related issues when in a social environment.
- ☐ Take any opportunity to increase your knowledge of the employee and their interests but always be mindful of their privacy rights. Openly share your own plans and activities if employees show interest.
- ☐ Actively participate in the organization's team-building exercises —and encourage staff to participate as well.
- ☐ Try to make the workplace relaxed and fun. Help organize social events and try to attend work-related social occasions.
- ☐ Provide space on the office network for employees to publish their personal web pages, showing their interests, favorite photographs, and so on. Use this space to publish your own personal information.
- ☐ Ensure that ongoing contact and communication is effective and efficient.

As your relationship with your staff becomes stronger, your ability to trust them will also increase—particularly if you also establish effective communication modes.

Step Four. Motivation: Developing and Building Trust and Mentoring

Qualifications and Skills

Managers already trust external examinations, agency processes, and trainers and their more experienced staff. And as a result they usually trust that the employee can do the job to the standards required, regardless of where they are located.

Follows are some suggestions to increase trust regarding qualifications/skills:

☐ Verify that external qualifications are appropriate and genuine.

☐ Ensure that all employees attend all relevant training courses and monitor the training sector to see whether there are new courses that might be more relevant and useful. Increasing staff qualifications can increase productivity, confidence, and performance.

☐ Review induction training to confirm that employees have all the necessary agency-specific information.

☐ Meet regularly with employees who have responsibilities as a 'buddy' or mentor for new employees to discuss their progress.

☐ "Test" the employee in a casual, nonthreatening manner. Ask questions that relate to specific skill sets, invent scenarios and see how he or she reacts, or expand duties on a short term basis to help them grow in their job.

☐ Allow staff to telework for a trial period to confirm that they can make it work effectively.

Coaching and Counseling

Managing for Excellence[13] defines coaching as "the art of improving the performance of others." For managers, this means encouraging team members to learn from and be challenged by their work, as well as creating conditions for continuous development by helping staff define and achieve goals.

In contrast, leadership involves knowing what is required and using the right approach—appropriate for both the circumstances and the people involved—enabling the team to gain its objective. At some point in our careers, most of us have used the wrong approach and paid the price for it. But the right approach in leadership can yield amazing results.

However, if you ask twenty people to define motivation, you are likely to receive as many different answers. Some people feel that the only true motivation comes from within, fueled by inspiration or the desire to succeed. Nevertheless, the manager can certainly help. In this context, motivation is best defined as the desire to accomplish a goal or participate in an endeavor.

While not always the case, there does seem to be a correlation between motivation and results. A motivated person usually achieves results or, put another way, achievement usually motivates.

---

13 Moi, Ali, et al. Managing for Excellence,(New York: DK, 2001) 222-7.

Coaching vs. Counseling

Coaching and counseling share many of the same skills and come down to the supervisor telling the employee what he/she wants done and how it should be done. To further define each:

- ☐ **Coaching** - A directive process by a manager to train and orient an employee to the realities of the workplace and to help the employee remove barriers toward optimum work performance.

- ☐ **Counseling** - A supportive process by the manager to help an employee define and work through problems affecting job performance. Therefore, dealing with an employee who lacks specific job knowledge would require strong coaching skills; while dealing with a problem employee will require good counseling skills. Knowing the difference between each and knowing when to use one over the other will help the manager in managing an employee's work product from a distance. Recently, coaching has become widespread in management and in many cases has replaced counseling, which can imply that the employee falls short of the agency's standard (hence the need for counseling) and is in some manner being penalized and reprimanded (if only in the nicest way). Coaching offers a more positive and encouraging approach. It helps level the playing field and provides an opportunity to ask open-ended questions and discover solutions mutually beneficial to all parties.

Other benefits include developing competence and confidence, easier diagnosis of problems in behavior and performance, and maintaining the dignity of team members. Coaching can also foster better working relationships in the group as employees begin to coach each other.

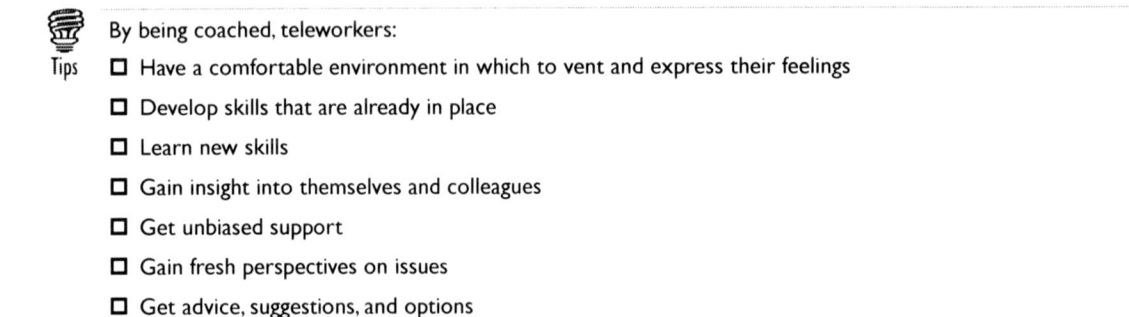

Tips

By being coached, teleworkers:
- ☐ Have a comfortable environment in which to vent and express their feelings
- ☐ Develop skills that are already in place
- ☐ Learn new skills
- ☐ Gain insight into themselves and colleagues
- ☐ Get unbiased support
- ☐ Gain fresh perspectives on issues
- ☐ Get advice, suggestions, and options

The downside of coaching is that it can take an inordinate amount of time, and when frustrated, managers may find themselves reverting the counseling or authoritative style of management. And due to the supervisory nature of management, employees will always be the subordinates – no amount of coaching can change that. Nevertheless, coaching can be used in many management and team-building situations, particularly when starting out with a telework

Step Four. Motivation: Developing and Building Trust and Mentoring

program. Early on, it sets the stage for performance and allows for rules that apply to everyone in the group, creating an atmosphere of fairness.

Managing for Excellence[14] offers a model of six basic stages for each goal to achieve when coaching:

- ☐ **Definition:** Determine performance goals (coach/person being coached must agree on goals.)
- ☐ **Analysis:** Define the current reality (What is the present position?).
- ☐ **Exploration:** Look at various options that will achieve goals
- ☐ **Action:** What tasks are needed to achieve goals (involves a commitment by all parties)

These four stages can sometimes be accomplished in a single coaching session. From there, the coachee goes onto the next step:

- ☐ **Learning:** The person being coached implements the agreed-upon action with the support of the coach (this can take considerable time, depending upon the goal or desired performance)
- ☐ **Feedback:** Review progress; determine what has been learned, and how the person being coached can build upon this knowledge to reach the next goal.

Effective Coaching

Effective coaching not only helps develop the skills and talents of each teleworker, but it gives the program momentum and offers a definable benchmark for goals as well as opportunities to set new goals. However, it does require effort on the part of the managers who will need to keep a positive attitude and set aside time for coaching, encourage team members to come up with new ideas and take responsibility for same, and offer support and resources to achieve various goals.

Tips

Listed below are some characteristics to effective coaching:

- ☐ Capitalize on the employee's strengths.
- ☐ Make performance expectations and priorities clear.
- ☐ Set standards of excellence while providing the employee the freedom to do the job.
- ☐ Hold employee accountable for his/her action/product.

After you have provided the coaching and you believe the employee has all the skills necessary to be a successful performer yet you still do not see the desired level of proficiency you may want to resort to counseling. This next step is very critical in laying the groundwork for identifying precisely where the employee is falling short in your expectations.

---

14 Managing for Excellence, 223

Handbook for Managing Teleworkers – Toolkit

Suggestions on Counseling

Tips

The following eleven steps to counseling an employee on his/her performance is neutral, direct and most importantly effective in dealing with early performance problems. Following these steps does not require any great skill in dealing with people; it is a simple technique that can be learned and applied by anyone.

1. Define your goal.

2. Relate your goal to the mission of the organization.

3. Plan in advance the topic, time and location of the discussion. Make sure the telecommuter is to be in the office the day of the meeting.

4. Be assertive rather than accusatory.

5. Acknowledge your own subjectivity.

6. Describe the performance problem succinctly.

7. Ask the employee for suggestions for improvement.

8. Outline specific corrective action to be taken, with specific time frames.

9. Ask the employee to summarize the discussion.

10. Schedule a follow-up meeting to discuss improvement (or lack of).

11. Listen more than talk.

Mentoring

A mentor is someone who shares knowledge, wisdom, and experience about his or her occupation or workplace. You may have had the fortunate experience of having one or more mentors during various stages of your career.

Mentoring is a more personal relationship than coaching. You've found someone (perhaps a younger, less experienced version of yourself) whom you feel holds great promise. So you want to help them along. Seeing them grow and develop professionally can be gratifying and rewarding to both of you. Mentoring also challenges your management style and helps you refine it as you teach it to others.

Checklist

According to the Small Business Administration[15] (SBA), mentors should do the following:

☐ Provide guidance based on past business experiences.

☐ Create a positive counseling relationship and climate of open communication.

☐ Help the protégé (mentee) identify problems and solutions.

☐ Lead the protégé through the problem-solving processes.

☐ Offer constructive criticism in a supportive way.

☐ Share stories, including mistakes.

---

15 "Lead :Mentoring" online article, Small Business Administration, nd (www.sba.gov/smallbusinessplanner/manage/lead/SERV_MENTORING.html}

98   www.GovernmentTrainingInc.com

Step Four. Motivation: Developing and Building Trust and Mentoring

- ☐ Assign "homework" if applicable.
- ☐ Refer the protégé to other business associates.
- ☐ Be honest about business expertise.
- ☐ Solicit feedback from the protégé.
- ☐ Come prepared to each meeting to discuss issues

The SBA also recommends being clear about how and when you'll help and understanding that the relationship will end (or take a different form) when the mentee moves on. At some point the mentee may resist your suggestions, and the relationship may encounter difficulties as you provide honest feedback. Mentors can only offer counseling to a point—the protégé needs to find his or her own path.

Managers should take time to mentor. Along with providing a sense of continuity, you have the reward of helping someone along with their career and passing along your knowledge and expertise. One of the most rewarding aspects of managing is being able to help individuals, whether it be coaching and guiding your team or nurturing someone you feel has a special talent in your area of expertise or workplace.

Effective Feedback

Feedback is an important aspect of a manager's arsenal. How a manager provides feedback is often the difference between success and failure. There are four types of feedback:

1. Silence or no response provided.

2. Criticism or the identification of behaviors or results that are undesirable or substandard.

3. Advice or identification of best practices and how to incorporate these practices in future products.

4. Reinforcement or identification of behaviors or results that are desired or exceed standards.

Certainly, the first two forms of feedback are the least desirable, but how do you give effective feedback? Listed below are some pointers.

- ☐ Make your feedback specific and performance related.
- ☐ Consider the timing, either before the event in the form of advice or immediately after the event as positive reinforcement.
- ☐ Consider the needs of the person receiving the feedback as well as your own needs. Are you "dumping" or genuinely trying to improve performance?
- ☐ Focus on behavior the receiver can do something about.

Tips

www.GovernmentTrainingInc.com

- ☐ Solicit feedback rather than impose it.
- ☐ Avoid labels and judgments by describing rather than evaluating behavior.
- ☐ Define the impact on you, the team, the unit, the organization.
- ☐ Use "I" statements rather than "You" statements to reduce defensiveness.
- ☐ Check to be sure clear communication has occurred.
- ☐ Give feedback in a calm, unemotional language. Pay specific attention to tone and body language.

Finally, there are six additional points to remember.

1. Reinforcement is the most effective form of feedback.

2. Criticism is the most ineffective form of feedback.

3. The difference between criticism and advice is a difference in timing. Most criticism can be given as advice.

4. Mixed feedback dilutes the impact. Most times it serves to confuse the employee.

5. Criticism will overpower all other types of feedback.

6. Silence is not always golden. Many times it can be left to a myriad of interpretations.

Performance Based Action: The Last Alternative

You have given clear direction; you have provided feedback; you have coached and counseled, but the employee's performance remains below acceptable standards. The next step is to initiate an appropriate performance based action. When faced with this alternative make sure you work closely with your employee relations specialist. The following provides options to consider when initiating a performance based action.

- ☐ **Opportunity to improve.** Otherwise known as the performance improvement period is the formal period of time the manager provides the employee to improve his/her performance. There are several factors associated with this phase:
  - Document every assignment given to the employee, and the employee's performance related to the critical element at issue.
  - Provide any advice, assistance, guidance, and counseling as specified in the opportunity Letter; document your efforts.
  - Keep all drafts through the final version of the work product.
  - Evaluate the evidence of the performance during the opportunity period.

Step Four. Motivation: Developing and Building Trust and Mentoring

- **Postponement or denial of within-grade-increase (WIGI).** This is usually done at the same time the employee is given an opportunity to improve his/her performance. Contrary to many employees' perception WIGI's are not based on longevity alone.
  - Employee must be notified in writing, at least 30 days before the WIGI is due.
  - Memorandum must contain specific reason(s) why the WIGI is postponed or denied.
  - Once performing satisfactorily the manager should notify the employee in writing and initiate the process for granting a WIGI.
- **Downgrade and reassignment to different position.** This allows the manager to retain an employee who can still be an asset to the organization, just not in his/her current position. Usually the employee is reassigned to a lower grade level.
  - This option is most commonly offered when an employee is promoted into a new position and his/her performance in the former position was satisfactory.
  - There is no requirement that a manager offer this option to an employee before considering termination.
- **Termination for poor performance.** This is usually the last resort to be considered when dealing with a poor performer. You, the manager, have made a decision the organization would be better off without this employee's services.
  - Consider alternatives to termination.
  - Offer the employee the option to resign rather than be removed for unacceptable performance.
  - Allow the employee a period of time to look for another job before the effective date of resignation.
  - Offer outplacement counseling, if available, through the Human Resources office.
  - Write a factual yet positive reference letter for the employee to use when looking for alternative employment.

These options are decided by the circumstances and are by no means mandatory. However, effective managers will use every option available to benefit themselves and the agency, as well as the under-performing employee.

Dealing With A Conduct Problem

Generally there are three reasons why employees do not get their job done. They are:

- The employee does not know how to do the job.
- There is something or someone that keeps the employee from getting the job done.
- The employee simply does not want to do the job.

Conduct problems are a result of a "won't do" rather than a "can't do". It is not a skills deficiency, but rather the employee knows how to perform the assigned task but for some reason refuses to do it. Therefore, conduct or behavior problems involve the breaking of a rule, regulation, or other requirement.

In the traditional office environment, employees can come to their manager with a specific problem or the manager sees the problem firsthand. In a remote relationship, the manager must learn to recognize signs of conduct or attitude problems.

The following are signs of declining performance:

☐ Decreased productivity
☐ Poor work quality
☐ Missed due dates
☐ Disorganization

The following are signs of attitudinal problems:

☐ Little or no initiative
☐ Disinterest
☐ Increased complaining
☐ Increased irritability or depression

Recognizing these signs will help you deal with them more effectively.

The first two steps to take in dealing with a conduct problem are similar to those for a performance problem.

1. Identify that there is a problem

2. Meet with the employee.

Tips

The purpose of the meeting with the employee is again similar to that with performance problems:
☐ Explain what the problem is.
☐ Explain why it is a problem.
☐ Explain what you expect the employee to do to correct the problem.
☐ Document your discussion.

If the employee still will not abide by the requirements, fairness to other employees in the work unit dictates that a manager take effective disciplinary action. The purpose of discipline is

Step Four. Motivation: Developing and Building Trust and Mentoring

to help supervisors maintain an efficient and productive work environment. It should be used to correct unacceptable conduct, not punish an employee. Therefore, the third step is:

3. Recommending an adverse/disciplinary action.

Before taking this step, ask yourself two questions. *Must Do*
- ☐ Was the rule communicated to the employee, or if not, is the offense so obvious that they could be expected to know without being told?
- ☐ Has the rule been consistently enforced in the past, and if not, were employees told that it was now going to be enforced before this incident occurred?

If you can answer "Yes" to either of these questions then you are ready to recommend an action.

Also, you will need to:

☐ Consider all the facts.

☐ Consider the employee's side of the story.

☐ Have a meaningful discussion with the employee relations (E/R) specialist.

☐ Recommend the proposed action to be taken.

If the employee continues to engage in the unacceptable behavior or conduct, then the action taken to correct the problem will become more severe after each instance. Maintain a discussion with your E/R specialist so that you have the advice you need.

Remember when dealing with conduct problems the characteristics of a successful disciplinary process should be: *Remember*
- ☐ Prompt
- ☐ Impartial
- ☐ Consistent
- ☐ Non-punitive
- ☐ Fair
- ☐ Advance warning
- ☐ Follow through

The Big Picture: Dos and Don'ts In Providing Support

Supervising teleworkers provides an opportunity to do things in a new and often better way. You may need some of the following adjustments:

☐ Maintain a sense of control even when people are out of sight.

☐ Develop increased levels of trust and use trust as a purposeful tool.

☐ Use technology for staying in touch with teleworkers.

☐ Rethink and redesign the way certain jobs are performed.

☐ Plan meetings and other team activities further in advance.

☐ Focus objectives and expectations on short-term, project-based goals.

☐ Adopt location-independent ways of measuring performance and results.

☐ Transition teamwork toward more electronic-based collaboration.

Also consider the following ways of providing support and motivation:

☐ Managing teleworkers by close, constant supervision isn't possible or desirable. Instead, manage primarily on the basis of results.

☐ Discuss in advance what you expect from teleworkers and be certain they understand the criteria you will be using to rate their performance.

☐ Track progress also by results.

☐ Be certain that teleworkers understand the deadlines for assignments and the resources required to meet them.

☐ Use planning skills to effectively distribute work so that offsite and onsite personnel are treated equally.

☐ Establish a regular means of communication to help clarify work expectations, deadlines, questions and important office developments.

☐ Set up a regular schedule of progress reviews.

☐ Use your time spent with teleworkers to coach and help develop their capabilities. Quickly reinforce positive behavior and bring unsatisfactory performance to the employee's attention. Maintain contact with offsite staff via voice mail, electronic mail, and teleconferences to provide timely, ongoing feedback.

If the arrangement isn't working out, it is OK to drop out of the program. Telework arrangements offer numerous benefits, but is not ideal for every job or every employee.

! Do

Must Do ☐ Trust your employees.

☐ Be certain that you and your employees complete any surveys, feedback forms, or other evaluations tools that your employer requests.

☐ Use your telework arrangement as a new way to optimize your managing skills.

Step Four. Motivation: Developing and Building Trust and Mentoring

- ☐ Manage by results. Results are what is important, not face-to-face time.
- ☐ Telework yourself when you have the opportunity. The experience will give you insight on the benefits and challenges of the arrangement.
- ☐ Try to see things from a teleworker's perspective.
- ☐ Keep your telework staff in mind when setting department goals.
- ☐ Delegate work fairly between teleworkers and nonteleworkers.
- ☐ Include teleworkers in daily activities. Keep an eye out for teleworkers who feel isolated.
- ☐ Encourage communication between teleworkers and nonteleworkers.

Don't
- ☐ Check on teleworkers every hour for status updates.
- ☐ Ignore your teleworkers.
- ☐ Set up unrealistic deadlines.
- ☐ Ignore problems.
- ☐ Neglect your teleworker.
- ☐ Set unreachable goals.
- ☐ Expect perfection–adjustments to your telework program are inevitable.
- ☐ Allow one unsuccessful teleworking experience to give the program a bad reputation.
- ☐ Expect everyone to be successful at teleworking.
- ☐ Make negative remarks about teleworkers or the telework program in front of office workers.
- ☐ Give preferential treatment, mentoring, and promotions to office workers.

Success Stories

Treasury Inspector General For Tax Administration (TIGTA)

TIGTA's telework program grew out of a task group that had been formed to make TIGTA a better place to work and to position the agency as an employer- of-choice. Every time the task group met, its members talked about wanting the flexibility to work from anywhere. "Telework just seemed to fit the bill," recalls Donna Leach, Human Resources Specialist & Telework Program Manager.

The task group talked with the inspector general (IG—the head of the agency) and proposed a pilot program. TIGTA itself was formed January 1999. The agency implemented its telework pilot in September 2000. The pilot was supposed to last nine to 12 months, but after six months the agency cut it short and made plans to move ahead. Program implementation began in August 2001.

Handbook for Managing Teleworkers – Toolkit

The Telework Experience

"There was so much change with TIGTA being new," recalls Leach, "but our upper level management and our IG were very supportive." The telework policy was restructured based on feedback received during the pilot, then the agency developed manager and employee training. The three-day manager training program focused on issues like: how to deal with employees, how to tell an employee he/she can't participate, how to deal with conduct and performance issues for remote employees, virtual teams, and more.

September 11, 2001 interrupted the training process, and the program was put on hold for the remainder of that year. The training began again in January 2002.

Part of the manager training involved putting the four managers who had participated in the pilot program at the podium, where they talked about their experiences. "On the whole, most were open to it but were not sure," says Leach. "One of the advantages was we already had employees spread out in offices around the U.S., and they already managed virtually. So we stressed managing deliverables rather than managing employees. If you manage products and deliverables you're going to know it if there's a problem."

The IT and human resources departments were very involved in setting up the program. "We had our IT people working with HR to help set up high-speed Internet access (either DSL or cable modem) at employees' homes," explains Leach. "We met weekly with IT staff to resolve problems as they arose, and we answered questions and provided support to make implementation as smooth as possible."

About 90 percent of TIGTA employees participated. Leach says as of April 2006, 17.85 percent of TIGTA employees telework four to five days a week; 24.35 percent telework two to three days a week; 5.91 percent telework one day a week; 39.83 percent participate on an episodic (task-related) basis; 4.73 percent are ineligible to telework (mostly due to the nature of their job, or in some cases performance issues); 6.97 percent choose not to participate. Leach gets detailed program stats because she asked her IT department to put a field in TIGTA's management information system that will track participation levels. She says the agency's audit staff has the most full-time participants, while the investigations division has the most "episodic" participants. Leach says participation has been such that no significant internal marketing efforts have been needed. The telework program is covered, however, as part of the new employee orientation just to let people know it's available.

Indeed, the program has been so popular that the agency uses it as a recruitment tool. TIGTA mentions the program in its vacancy announcements, highlighting telework as one of its employee benefits. "We don't say you can telework as soon as you're hired, though," notes Leach. "We recommend people wait six months before requesting permission to telework."

Step Four. Motivation: Developing and Building Trust and Mentoring

Leach credits the telework program for aiding employee retention, although she notes that her evidence is anecdotal. "We have a fairly low attrition rate," she reports. Moreover, positive responses to the program have been fairly high on the two telework-related questions asked in the agency's employee satisfaction survey.

Challenges and Investment

TIGTA combined the implementation of its telework program with an agency-wide technology upgrade, moving all employees from desktop to laptop computers — which it leased instead of purchased.

Security costs were built in across the board.

For employees who telework two or more days a week, the agency pays half the cost of broadband

Internet installation and access; gives them a multiport router (which allows them to access the Internet separately for personal versus government use); and gives them a printer. Full-time teleworkers get an agency-paid second phone line and a locking file cabinet.

"We had minimal outlay, the way we structured this," explains Leach. "We reserved $400,000, and it didn't cost a quarter of that."

Other than some employee frustrations in setting up their broadband connections, Leach says the only obstacles in launching the telework program "were the normal things that can happen when you change something. There's an agitated state at the time when you're making changes. When we were setting it up, the IG was so behind the program that it helped things go smoothly."

Program Outlook

"I don't think we'll ever go back," predicts Leach. She says the program has been so successful that the agency has taken it to the next level: hoteling. "One of our executives went to our Atlanta office and noticed a lot of empty desks," she explains. The agency realized the large number of teleworkers there enabled it to get rid of some space. Then it looked at its Dallas location — with the same result. "When one of our executives or a real estate analyst sees that we have excess space, or when a space is scheduled for renovation, we look at how many teleworkers we have and see if we can cut back on leased space," says Leach. "We thought we would save approximately $100,000 in Atlanta, but then rent went up, so we might have saved only about $50,000. The balance would be attributable to cost avoidance rather than savings."

The space reductions allowed them to avoid tapping program budgets to cover increased rents. Moreover, the agency has to zero-out the cost of office renovations in the same year they're incurred, so the savings from teleworking helps absorb those costs.

"Without a strong telework program you can't have hoteling, so we look at this as phase two of our telework program," says Leach. She anticipates that telework will become part of TIGTA's continuity of operations plan (COOP), and that hoteling will be expanded to more locations.

Most Helpful Resources

TIGTA initially drew some telework lessons from major IT corporations, says Leach, but networking has become the best resource as more Federal agencies have adopted programs. She speaks highly of quarterly meetings hosted by the Office of Personnel Management (OPM) for teleworking agencies, which gives coordinators a chance to talk with one another.

Success Tips
- Put a policy in place and then do it. Start with a formal pilot, and have a policy for it.
- Based on the pilot results, monitor everything, make your changes, and implement the program.
- Don't worry about everything.
- Communication is a big part of the program; employees need to communicate with managers and vice versa.
- Training is also very important.

Copyright © 2006 Commuter Connections/Metropolitan Washington Council of Governments

U.S. Postal Service Office of Inspector General

The U.S. Postal Service Office of Inspector General (OIG), an independent agency within the Postal Service, employs more than 1,100 auditors, investigators, and professional support staff located in more than 90 offices nationwide. The OIG plays a key role in maintaining the integrity and accountability of America's postal service, its revenue and assets, and its employees. With $73 billion in revenue, the Postal Service is at the core of a $900 billion mailing industry that employs more than nine million people. The more than 700,000 employees of the Postal Service comprise the largest civilian Federal workforce in the country.

In December 2004, the OIG launched an advanced telework policy, named Smart Workplace (SWP), as part of an overall effort to focus on the management of work assignments — not just the management of employees. This policy provides greater flexibility for OIG employees to perform their jobs where it makes the most sense, including outside of their assigned duty station.

The "Smart Work" Experience

The Smart Workplace program enables OIG staff to perform their assigned duties at optimal locations, including those outside of their regularly assigned duty station. Smart Workplace allows employees to "work smarter" by working wherever it makes the most sense based on their assignments. Inherent with the program's flexibility is the option to telework. Flexibility from both managers and employees is critical to the success of SWP. There are organizational or business

Step Four. Motivation: Developing and Building Trust and Mentoring

needs that require individuals to be present at an assigned duty station and in those instances they are to provide appropriate notification and communication accordingly.

Challenges and Investment

In 2006, the OIG's Smart Workplace program was deemed successful and given the Telework Award by Commuter Connections. In mid-2008, an advisory council of managers and employees from across the OIG convened to re-examine the program. They discussed how to enhance the submission process and address concerns from managers and employees alike. One concern raised was the inconsistent application of some aspects of the policy. The council's general consensus was to formalize and standardize the process for submitting and approving Smart Work requests. The council believed this would result in consistency and enable monitoring. They also recommended utilizing new technologies to place the program online, to streamline and automate the process.

In September 2008 a smaller focus group of council members met and prompted the following SWP program enhancements:

- ☐ The policy supporting the program was updated to clarify and formalize the process of 'Smart Working,' and included a reporting function to better gauge consistent application across the agency and to measure program effectiveness.
- ☐ In conjunction with policy revisions, the council created an action plan calling for continuous communications from the highest levels of leadership to the managers and employees out in the field.
- ☐ Online tutorials walking through the process of filling out and reviewing plans to Smart Work were launched.
- ☐ Additional training is planned for later this year, and initial data from the reporting function will be analyzed to determine usage and indicators of improved performance trends.
- ☐ An online request form was created to track employee and manager accountability. It links to an automated calendar housed in the OIG's intranet portal — the Knowledge Centered Environment (KCE). The calendar (Consolidated Calendar) connects to various applications that track Leave, Training, and Travel. Now Smart Workplace information is displayed to both managers and employees at their team level allowing an at-a-glance indication of business activities to the individual and his or her management.

Whenever an employee submits a plan to work away from their duty station, their manager receives an e-mail notification to review the plan. A form was designed to capture minimum information — such as the date and time of the requested SWP plan. Optional fields include alternate contact information such as a phone or e-mail address. The simplicity of the form and the automated e-mail notifications were intended to help keep the administrative burden to a minimum for both the individual and manager. Requests that are denied are also tracked. Smart

Work arrangements may be denied due to the need for face-to-face meetings or other business reasons that require the employee to report to their office.

After input from senior leadership, the legal department, council representatives, and the Inspector General, the policy was formally updated in April 2009. The revised policy and reporting functions enable managers and employees to approach SWP with more balance. The policy further clarifies manager and employee responsibilities when Smart Working, and even provides guidance for exceptional circumstances including limitations on employees whose work necessitates their presence at their assigned duty station. Open discussions between employees and managers about the best way to apply SWP, along with clear directions on assignments and expectations, are prerequisite to the submission of any SWP plans.

Program Outlook

The OIG's revised SWP policy and advancements in SWP tracking usage is timely and progressive in light of the two telework bills introduced before Congress -- The Telework Improvements Act (H.R. 1722) and The Telework Enhancement Act (S. 707) – proposing updated standards for telework. Once the initial usage tracking data is analyzed, the OIG believes the reporting and flexibility of use across the organization will further validate the improvements, and show a return on investment in terms of continuity of operations, continually increased productivity, and improved employee satisfaction.

The OIG faces the same human capital crisis as other government agencies, with the majority of employees coming from the "Baby Boomer" generation who are eligible for retirement in the next 5 to 10 years. Increased flexibility to work remotely is a privilege many of the Millennial generation consider highly valuable when seeking employment, and will assist OIG efforts to remain a competitive employer with other Federal agencies and the private sector.

Most Helpful Resources

The OIG's Smart Workplace program owes much to the Inspector General, as the program's initial sponsor in 2004, and through his continued support for enhancements. The feedback from employees and managers, especially those from the September of 2008 council focus group meeting, was invaluable in identifying opportunities for program enhancements.

The OIG's Information Technology team customized the online calendar and reporting to provide the increased accountability necessary to truly gauge the program's participation and outcomes. The revisions also relied on guidance from our legal office on the specific wording of the policy itself. Ultimately, support and promotion from the agency's executive management will be key to successful communication and program effectiveness.

Step Four. Motivation: Developing and Building Trust and Mentoring

Success Tips

To achieve similar telework results along the line of a Smart Workplace, the OIG recommends:

- ☐ Benchmarking with other agencies that perform similar functions.
- ☐ Solicit feedback from within all levels of the organization.
- ☐ Keep the rules simple as possible to provide guidance but allow for exceptions.
- ☐ Obtain communication support from leadership.
- ☐ Provide training and support on both the policy and associated tracking tools.

Above all else, trust in the professionalism of staff members is integral to successful telework programs!

STEP FIVE. VIRTUAL TEAMS AND CHANGE MANAGEMENT

Virtual teams have been defined by authors Stevie Peterson and Velda Storr as a "group of individuals who work across time, space, and organizational boundaries with links strengthened by webs of communication technology. They have complementary skills and are committed to a common purpose, have interdependent performance goals, and share an approach to work for which they hold themselves mutually accountable."[16] Such teams allow organizations to hire and retain the most qualified people regardless where they are located.

However, virtual teams and teleworkers are not mutually exclusive. The latter is confined to individuals who work from home whereas virtual teams can consist of employees who work either at home and/or at one or more offices in different areas.

> **Remember**
> Today's global environment, with its continued shift from production to service/knowledge increasingly places less emphasis on physical location. While there will always be a use for office workers and manufacturing facilities, many companies have turned to "outsourcing" of individuals or groups. Tasks assigned to virtual teams range from the more routine, such as customer care to highly specialized design or computer programming. The bottom line for creating a virtual team is that in order for the job to get done you don't need everybody physically there to do it.

Developing The Team

Teamwork is important in many businesses and need not be an obstacle. After all, there are many types of teams—and most already have a 'virtual' element. An orchestra is a team of musicians. They meet to perform together a dozen or more times a year, they meet in sections (brass, violins, etc.) to practice and rehearse, they play together in quartets of chamber ensembles and they practice on their own. A teleworker, on his or her telework days, is similar to the musician who is practicing on his or her own before rejoining one of the larger combinations when back in the office. A sports team is a team of athletes. They also perform together, train together or in smaller groups and also follow their own personal fitness programs, away from the rest of the team.

---

16 Peterson, Stevie and Storr, Velda. "Why Virtual Teams?" online article, 2000 (www.managementhelp.org/grp_skll/virtual/defntion.pdf).

Teams also have different purposes, goals, and organizational setup. Some teams might train together but then work totally on their own for a shared objective. Other teams might meet only once or twice a year for a conference or team building event, spending the rest of their time working largely on their own. A travelling sales force is one example. Still other teams will never meet, such as an engineering consultancy firm designing and building an oil refinery with designers in Houston and Singapore, management in Perth and London, operational staff in Singapore and Delhi, and day-to-day management on site outside Mumbai.

Remember Individuals, including managers, sustain each of these teams. They show collective responsibility for the shared objectives and also understand their individual responsibilities. Each team also relies on the organization's support for their success. This support is demonstrated by ensuring that the organization's culture is appropriate, leadership is effective, staff training and skills are adequate, appropriate processes and workflows have been developed, and that the technology used is supportive.

Another characteristic of successful teams, whether virtual or not, is the recognition that the team process is all about relationships and shared values. It is important to assess the makeup and characteristics of the team and to incorporate the organization's values when planning activities and agreements. Team relationships should be based on centralized knowledge, streamlined knowledge transfer, and clear communication processes that help to align expectations. Relationships also require transparent and consistent communication and use of information and the involvement of all team members in developing solutions. Sound relationships and shared team values can help prevent a breakdown in effective working arrangements.

Types of Virtual Teams

There are several types of virtual teams. Your telework initiative may fit one or more of these definitions, but understanding how they work and their differences can help you define how to set up your own team.

Networked

According to authors Deborah Duarte and Nancy Tennant Snyder,[17] networked teams typically cross time, distance, and organizational boundaries and lack a clear definition between the team and the organization. "Membership is frequently diffuse and fluid, with team members rotating on and off... as their expertise is needed." In fact, the structure of this type of team is so loosely based that its members may not even be aware of everyone who is in the network. Team members may be drawn, on a permanent or part-time basis, from universities, think tanks, corporations, or even different countries.

---

17 Duarte, Deborah and Snyder, Nancy Tennant. Mastering Virtual Teams, 3rd ed. (San Francisco: Jossey Bass, 2006): 4-9

Step Five. Virtual Teams and Change Management

Networked teams can be found in consulting firms and high-tech organizations, such as research and development companies who need specialized expertise or problem-solving where "discovery processes usually [don't]reside in a single location or organization," the authors continue. For example, if a healthcare certification firm was assigned to define best practices for its member hospitals, and the agency did not have the information on hand, they could utilize their various partners and databases as a resource to obtain the information.

Parallel

Like the Special Forces or Navy Seals, parallel teams "carry out special assignments, tasks, or functions that the regular organization does not want..or is not equipped to perform," the authors go on. These types of teams are utilized when the skill required cannot be found in the organization or particular location. As with networked teams, they cross time, distance, and organizational boundaries, but unlike them, have a distinct membership that sets it apart from the rest of the agency. Everyone knows who is on the team and they work closely to achieve a short-term goal or specific improvement. These teams are often found in multinational and global organizations when there is a need to define and provide a broad overview of worldwide processes and systems.

For instance, say a large computer manufacturer wants to define and set up a global order and customer satisfaction system. Members of the virtual parallel team would be drawn from various regions around the US and foreign countries. Team members would independently perform data collection and analysis through interviews and other market research, sometimes even using outside consultants to gather pertinent information. They would then report to the COO or individual overseeing the project via telephone or Internet conferences at a specific time and date, perhaps even using an interactive Web site. Once the project was completed and the goal achieved, the team would be disbanded.

Project/Product

> Like the first two types of teams, project or product development teams cross time, distance, and organizational boundaries. And like parallel teams they are assigned with the task of conducting or developing a specific project. Similar to networked teams, people move off and on the team as their expertise is required. Yet they are unique in several important ways: the focus is on a new product, information system, or organizational process and they are set up for a longer period, and may even be allowed to make decisions as opposed to recommendations. Members are also clearly delineated and with goals or products precisely set forth.

Remember

Project/product teams are likely to be found in companies developing a specific product or technology or engaging in scientific research. Along with having a great deal of influence and potential impact, this type of team utilizes a variety of resources to create new offerings or projects that can provide a competitive edge.

Production

Also known as work or functional teams, production teams perform more routine or ongoing types of tasks. They have a particular purpose such as training, research, accounting, and so forth. Traditionally, many were office workers, but today they can also be telecommuters, operating virtually and crossing boundaries of time and distance. These types of teams are often located, whether virtually or in real time, in global call or business centers and operate around the clock so they can provide service to customers 24/7.

As telecommuters, they have access to the agency's Intranet, so they can log on any time and document their activities/goals. They may meet face-to-face during training or for conferences, but even this may be done virtually.

Service

This type of team is self-explanatory and provides support or technical assistance. They may work around-the-clock dealing with problems and providing help, passing along any unresolved workload and issues to the next shift. Located anywhere and available whenever needed, they are distributed across distance and time. Many times finding individuals with specialized technical expertise from a single geographical area is nearly impossible. So you'll need to be able to recruit from all over the US to fill the spaces for this type of team.

Management

Like service teams, they too can be disbursed across distance and time. However, they work collaboratively, often on a daily basis to achieve corporate objectives and goals via audio and video conferences as well as through e-mail and other forms of electronic messaging. Duarte and Snyder provide the example of the U.S. Army Chief of Staff, which is run as a virtual team. "Staff members communicate regularly via e-mail and use an [Internet]chat room… to discuss important issues as they arise." Security and COOP plans are especially important for these types of teams.

Action

These teams are what they say—they offer immediate responses, many times to an emergency. Crossing distance and organizational boundaries, their membership may be fluid. A national or international news organization is a good example of an action team (in fact, that's what they often call themselves). They have regular reporters or anchors and also use area correspondents or "stringers" for specific locations. Along with the camera crew or photographers who send images and film, they provide information which is transmitted to the editor and thus disseminated to the public via print or broadcast.

Step Five. Virtual Teams and Change Management

Ensuring Success of The Virtual Team
- Many of the same principles that apply to managing teleworkers also pertain to virtual teams. For instance, they should:
- Meet both management's and employees' needs.
- Consider the work habits and the job tasks to be completed.
- Utilize and develop telework agreements to provide a clear understanding of the key terms and conditions of the work arrangements.
- Manage all employees by results, whether teleworkers or not. Focus on the final product rather than processes used to produce it.
- Use collaboration to set work schedules. Develop work plans and task schedules based on input from the entire team.
- Be specific about what, where, when, and to what degree the work will be completed.
- Work to keep communication flowing between teleworkers, office workers, and customers.
- Monitor teleworkers' productivity, using a variety of measures.
- Ensure that technology requirements are identified and addressed.

Change Management

Telework is a natural outgrowth of the new challenges and demands presented by a knowledge-based economy. These changes affect everyone, regardless of their position in the organization. Some people will adapt easily, while others regard change as immensely threatening. As a manager, the challenge is to find a way to implement change with a minimum of stress.

Suggestions for Dealing with Change

Even though you can't entirely predict the impact of change, you can prepare yourself and your employees by doing the following:

- Plan
    - Plan ahead whenever possible. The first question on most employees' minds is "How is this going to affect me?" Dropping hints or providing vague answers can cause unnecessary anxiety and make the change more difficult to accept. So try to have as much information about the change as possible before introducing it to workers. The more organized you appear the more they will trust not only you, but the change itself.
- Communicate
    - Communication is always important, even more so when you face change. A lack of communications from others can have a negative impact, while effective communications can have the reverse effect. You need details about the change, so be proactive -- Talk to your boss, your boss's boss, and so forth and get as much information as possible. When dealing with employees, however, be aware that news regarding the change may become distorted and mixed with rumor.

◇ Also remember that communication goes both ways. While you are providing employees with information about the change, invite their communication, feedback, and questions as well. Everyone, no matter what their position in the organization, wants to be heard and feel that their concerns and ideas are valued. Also, the more information they have, the more comfortable they will feel and more likely they will be to accept the change.

◇ Especially during times of change, make sure you're available to employees. They will have questions, especially at the beginning. Knowing that you can address their concerns can help them feel more secure and confident about their roles.

☐ Follow Up

◇ Following up with employees to see how they're doing is key to implementing any successful change. What kind of impact has the change had on their job? Are any adjustments needed or have there been any unexpected outcomes? Plan to follow up with employees on a regular basis; their cooperation and feedback is essential in ensuring positive outcomes.

☐ Listen

◇ Whether or not you agree with what they're saying, listen to your employees. Again this is especially vital during times of change – not only are they on the "front lines" of seeing where problems may surface, they may also have suggestions to make a process run smoother. Employees are a source of great ideas and positive employee/manager relations and interactions will help make your (and their) job easier and more effective during times of change.

The Four Dynamics of Change

Most people follow certain developmental phases when dealing with change. These phases are similar to the five phases discussed by the late Elizabeth Kubler-Ross in her book, On Death and Dying. Kubler-Ross's stages -- Denial, Anger, Bargaining, Depression, and Acceptance – have been applied to just about every form of personal loss or change, from death to divorce to addiction to even positive situations, such as a promotion.

Based on the Kubler-Ross model and applying it to the workplace, the four phases most people go through when confronted with change are:

1. Betrayal

2. Denial

3. Identity Crisis

4. Search for Solutions

As Kubler-Ross herself has noted, the phases do not always occur in sequential order, nor are they all experienced by every individual (although most people go through at least two).

Understanding the four developmental phases will help you define behaviors in yourself and others when faced with change in the workplace. Once you recognize these behaviors, you can deal

Step Five. Virtual Teams and Change Management

with them objectively, rather than allowing feelings to have a negative impact on your work and the agency.

Everyone goes through the phases at their own pace and at different times. For some people it takes a day; for others a week; and still others a couple of months. Some people never get over it and remain stuck in identity crisis or denial, despite your best efforts. But the faster you recognize which phase you're in (or which phase others are in), the better you can move on to the next one (or help others move on). And that's the key to getting through a particular change.

Betrayal

Feelings of betrayal crop up when someone or something that you count on and need seems to have let you down. Reactions range from feeling aghast and horrified to not knowing what to do or say to experiencing a sense of shock and numbness. Betrayal can take many forms and can be a matter of perception. For example, an employee who's been downsized or transferred to a less desirable job may feel a deep sense of injustice while the manager may merely see it as a cost-cutting measure or more effective way to do business.

Denial

Denial, the second stage, occurs when you move into disbelief. You can't, don't, and won't believe it. This is the phase where you begin to suffer and start feeling anxiety and pain concerning the change. The change makes you uncomfortable and your main interest at this point might be wanting to preserve the status quo.

Follows are some examples of denial.

- ☐ This isn't going to work.
- ☐ This doesn't apply to us because we are different/special/unique.
- ☐ This too shall pass.
- ☐ Things will stay the same, they'll work through the crisis/let me keep my office.
- ☐ I will believe it when I see it.
- ☐ Even if it happens it won't affect me.
- ☐ Here we go again.
- ☐ It's the management program du jour.
- ☐ This will blow over. It always does.
- ☐ We tried this two years ago and it didn't work then. So how can it possibly work now?
- ☐ And the old standby, "If I keep quiet and do my job, things will soon return to normal."

Somewhere after the changes are rolled out or announced or it becomes apparent that yes indeed, this is the way things will be done from now on. And that is when people move out of betrayal and into denial. If denial continues, productivity will keep spiraling downward.

Identity Crisis

Once you move out of denial, it's onto the third and often painful stage, the identity crisis, and the one in which anger and self-analysis come into play. The identity crisis is a lot like adolescence. People can become self-centered, opinionated, know-it-all, moody, overly sensitive, and quick to anger.

You and your employees may resist changes: "Why should I do this?" "I've worked hard for this agency and this is my reward?" Now the anger starts coming out, and with it a sense of withdrawal and lack of concentration. However, the anger is acceptable because your feelings are the bridge that will take you over to the next part of the identity crisis stage: Self-analysis.

Remember During self-analysis people start asking themselves a lot of questions:
- When will I fit in all this extra work?
- Will I be able to adapt?
- What am I going to do?
- Will I have the resources and training needed to get through this?
- Are they setting me up to get rid of me?
- Will I be able to handle the workload?
- It is even worth for me to continue to come in and fight these battles?
- And finally, the elephant in the living room: Do I really want to be part of this organization any more?

Search for Solutions

Search for solutions is the fourth and last stage. It may take some time – how long no one can predict exactly – but once you get there, only then can you begin to see the gain or the advantage in the change. Usually you don't get to this point until you've gone through the first three stages. And even then you may feel overwhelmed: "How am I going to get this all done?" "Who is responsible for what these days?" "This new system has me completely confused. Call the Geek Squad or get me some training!"

Here are some comments you might hear from employees in this phase:
- Let's do this thing.
- Let's get started.
- How about this? Here's an idea.

Step Five. Virtual Teams and Change Management

- ☐ This isn't as bad as I thought.
- ☐ Can we try this?
- ☐ That could work!

Remarks like these that means people are on board, willing to try the change, and accepting that it's here to stay (for now). According to some estimates, during a transition or in times of change, productivity can be cut by almost half thanks to gossip and speculation via water cooler gatherings, phone conversations, and even e-mail. Everything accelerates except for completion of work, despite the fact that getting it done has become even more crucial now that the change is underway.

> **Remember**
> There is no right or wrong pace in dealing with and adapting to change. But it's important to realize that change is inevitable: No matter what you do or where you work, certainly you are faced with some sort of change. So sit down and take a moment to assess whether you're at the beginning of the process – dealing with a sense of betrayal – or towards the end and accepting and adapting to the new way of doing things.

But more important than knowing where you are is understanding where you need to get to successfully deal with change. It's OK to be in betrayal and denial for a while, but realize that you need to move through these changes to get to the next level and complete the adjustment process.

So, you may think, what is the point of having a better understanding of how this process works? Change is still difficult and painful. Yet as you move through the process you learn about it and gain experience. In fact, the more awareness you have of the process, the more adept you become at dealing with it.

Change and Emotional Intelligence

> **Tips**
> Allowing emotions to control decisions can be detrimental, especially in the workplace, and particularly during times of change. Without a good grasp and understanding of their feelings, people often manifest anger in counterproductive behavior. You can help lessen anxiety by increasing emotional intelligence (EI). In a nutshell EI is the ability, to identify, assess, and manage the emotions of one's self, of others, and of groups and is especially useful when managers are confronted with difficult situations -- such as change. Through EI, you can help others recognize their own feelings and understand that they ultimately have control over their own lives. Along with an open-door policy whereby they can come to you during certain times with questions, encourage employees to reduce stress and anger through enjoyable outlets such as sports, hobbies, and increased family time.

"Effectively managing the workplace… means not fearing or resisting change and challenges, but empowering management and employees with the necessary skills to effectively manage life changes," observes Ida Covi, in "Leading the Workplace Within" on www.businessknowhow.com. While change is rarely easy, strategically preparing managers and employees will certainly help implement it more smoothly.

Success Story

Defense Information Systems Agency (DISA)

The (DISA) is a combat support agency responsible for planning, engineering, acquiring, fielding, and supporting global net-centric solutions to serve the needs of the President, Vice President, the Secretary of Defense, and other DoD Components, under all conditions of peace and war.

DISA's teleworking program was established in 2001 and was successful in meeting OPM's requirement to have all the employees in eligible positions offered the opportunity to telework. However, the DISA policy allowed employees to telework a maximum of one day every two week pay period. As the result of the 2005 DISA Employee Satisfaction survey, a recommendation was made to expand DISA's telework program. On December 21, 2005, the DISA Director changed the policy to allow employees to telework a maximum of two days per week, totaling four days per pay period.

During the same time period, DISA was selected under the Base Realignment and Closure Committee recommendations for relocation of its Headquarters function in Northern Virginia to Fort Meade, Maryland. Northern Virginia area, a solid strategy was needed for retention of this experienced, highly qualified workforce as well as one for recruitment of exceptionally qualified employees for the Fort Meade location. It was determined that the expansion of the telework program would serve as an excellent tool for both retention and recruitment. The successful implementation of the newly expanded telework program required extensive cultural change within all levels of management.

The Telework Experience

In January 2008, the DISA Director expanded the telework policy to three days per week, with supervisor approval. DISA's telework participation has increased ten-fold since the initial expansion of the telework policy. Currently DISA has over 2500 employees with approved telework applications for regular and recurring telework (at least once a pay period) and "ad hoc" (typically once a month).

Annual employee satisfaction surveys reveal a steady increase in satisfaction regarding DISA's quality of work life programs that was directly related to the telework program. Employees are now provided an opportunity to improve their quality of work life, save money due to reduced transportation cost and help improve the environment. Employees and managers have also recognized an increase in productivity in most instances. Under its policy, DISA furnishes government equipment for teleworking, consisting of a laptop and docking station. DISA has also implemented measures to access productivity for employees while teleworking through optional work plans.

Step Five. Virtual Teams and Change Management

DISA's policy authorizes reimbursement for high speed internet cost for regular and recurring teleworking employees. Telework is also an essential COOP enabler. As an enabler of our COOP, emergencies and inclement weather no longer cause lost productivity with employees now able to be as productive at home when needed. DISA is setting the standard for an effectively managed and maintained telework program for the Federal government. Telework has become an established way of doing business within DISA. DISA's telework program is not limited to the National Capitol Region and has been embraced by elements worldwide. Approximately 45 percent of the agency's workforce teleworks to some extent.

Successful implementation of the program allows DISA to work toward and achieve the following objectives: Facilitate BRAC relocation to Fort Meade, Maryland; improve employee productivity; improve retention and recruitment; ensure continuity of operations during emergencies. The program will also help to promote DISA as an "Employer of Choice"; Enhance DISA's efforts in employing and accommodating people with disabilities, reduce traffic congestion, decrease energy consumption and pollution emissions, and reduce parking congestion, transportation cost and costs of transit subsidies.

With the implementation of the noted effort above, DISA is now recognized as one of the leading Federal agencies in telework.

DISA has won four awards from the Telework Exchange, a public-private partnership focused on demonstrating the tangible value of telework and serving the emerging educational and communication requirements of the Federal telework community. In 2007, DISA was the only DoD element cited in a testimony before a Senate Committee covering positive examples of telework within the Federal government. DISA's Telework program was also selected for OPM's Chief Human Capital Officers (CHCO) Council's first Collection of Human Capital Practices for the Federal human resource community

Challenges and Investment

With the new policy in effect, several initiatives were implemented to leverage DISA's use of telework as both a recruitment and retention tool. These initiatives include:

- A "SWAT" team, was charged with researching best practices at other organizations, determining what equipment was needed, developing training needed for management and the workforce, and bringing it all together within 90 days. A senior HR manager and a senior IT manager co-chaired the SWAT team, blending the two critically needed functions together during the entire process, reducing potential problems or issues. There was also a change in acquisition policy regarding computer life cycle replacement computer equipment; DISA now uses a 90 percent laptop to 10 percent PC ratio. DISA also pays for 50 percent of the broadband cost on a monthly basis into teleworking employees' homes.

☐ Training was developed, specific to the culture of DISA, and provided to management at all levels as well as the workforce. In an effort to continually improve the program, training continues to be provided, including the creation of a computer based training (CBT) offering and instructor lead sessions "on demand." The training helps combat the fear factors managers and supervisors may experience prior to and during telework.

☐ An innovative web-based application was developed to support the Telework program, which allows employees to register for the telework program and select the adhoc or regular and recurring days they would like to work remotely. Managers are notified of pending applications and can login into this application to approve, disapprove, or modify their subordinates' registration requests. Additionally, managers can run reports which provide much needed data to assist in the Agency's management of the program.

DISA established its own telework centers at six (6) locations and continues to explore additional sites. DISA also continues to partner with OPM and GSA in exploring the possibility of establishing telework centers that will accommodate employees requiring access to the classified network.

Program Outlook

The telework SWAT team was established to forecast the way ahead for the telework program office. Although nothing has been set in stone they have made several recommendations for the program as we prepare for our move to Fort Meade Maryland. A listing of the recommended initiatives are:

☐ Exploring the possibility of establishing telework centers that will accommodate employees requiring access to the classified network

☐ Including managers in the telework program

Most Helpful Resources

To assist DISA in making the telework program successful, it was instrumental for all managers and supervisors to be on board with the program. The telework program office provided training for managers and supervisor within each directorate on the policies and procedures of DISA's telework program. They also expressed to reluctant managers the benefits of teleworking, so they could adapt with the changes of their employees not physically located at their official duty station. Through the training, managers were able to express their concerns and successes of allowing their employees to telework. If it weren't for managers taking the initiative and adapting to the changes in this ever changing environment the program would not be a success.

Step Five. Virtual Teams and Change Management

Success Tips
- ☐ The benefits of telework to both our employees and agency are listed below:
- ☐ Increased employee productivity
- ☐ Increases in retention, recruitment, and employee satisfaction are directly attributed to DISA's teleworking program
- ☐ Improved quality of life, job satisfaction and transportation cost reduction
- ☐ The ability to have a large portion of the workforce continue to be available and productive during emergency situations

Appendix I

Benefits of Telework

Employees who telework are often more productive and generate better quality work due to the quiet environment where interruptions are minimized.

Supervisors experience improved employee loyalty and commitment. Supervisors often report seeing an increase in quality of work and cooperation from the employee in ensuring that office coverage is maintained. In short, employees want to perpetuate the benefit they have been given.

Employees avoid arduous commutes to high-density urban areas, thus having more productive time available to carry out work assignments as opposed to sitting in traffic. This reduces employee stress levels, which in turn, contributes to better employee health.

Less commuting improves the environment by reducing air pollution.

In this increasingly competitive job market telework allows supervisors to attract and retain high quality employees.

Telework provides organizations with opportunities to test their Continuity of Operations Plans (COOP) on an on-going, day-to-day basis, allowing for bugs to be worked out of the COOP by providing support to alternative work-sites.

Managers can target specific labor markets such as handicapped individuals. Technological advances enable managers to support the disabled person with equipment that accommodates the individual's impairment, as well as permits flexibility in the location of the worksite.

Employees who are injured, recuperating, and/or physically limited may be able to work at home and complete work assignments while minimizing sick leave.

Telework has also been linked to reducing absenteeism, reducing training dollars by reducing employee turnover, as well as reducing parking issues and workspace issues in the office and long-term real estate costs.

Continuity of Operations (COOP)

FPC 65 is a government-wide initiative mandated by the President that was created to ensure the ability of the Federal Departments and Agencies to fulfill their essential roles and functions in response to a wide spectrum of threats. Each Department is required to develop and maintain a Continuity of Operations (COOP) Plan to ensure that mission essential function are operational within 12 hours of any emergency activation with or without warning. Some threats might include:

- ☐ Fire in the building
- ☐ Natural Disasters
- ☐ Threat or occurrence of terrorist attack
- ☐ Any event that makes it impossible for employees to work in their regular facility

Telework can be an essential part of a COOP. A fully implemented telework program should be a key component of an effective COOP Plan. Telework provides a cost effective reliable COOP capability that is routinely exercised since it is integrated into existing IT infrastructures and normal employee activities. To make telework a viable option during emergencies work must be organized to facilitate electronic communication and eliminate paper-based processes whenever possible, e.g., automating reports and procedures as much as possible. To facilitate the use of telework during emergencies Departments and their Components should:

Identify essential functions that essential personnel or key personnel can perform from a telework location. These employees should be familiar and comfortable in working from remote locations.

- ☐ Ensure the IT infrastructure can support the volume of telecommuting anticipated in an emergency.
- ☐ Permit essential personnel to work offsite at a designated telework site on a quarterly basis to test the worksite.
- ☐ Identify problems and develop new processes for accomplishing regular tasks from remote locations.
- ☐ Work through IT issues that arise from dealing with a variety of remote locations with a variety of equipment.
- ☐ Develop emergency training and exercises for essential "telework" personnel.
- ☐ Include agency telework coordinators in disaster planning.

Help Department decision makers understand that telework is an important agency tool, not just a "nice to have" flexibility for employees. Educate Component managers on the advantages of telework and how it would be beneficial in their emergency planning.

Consider scenarios where power is unavailable or certain regions or locations are inaccessible during various emergency situations. Then work backward to ensure that your COOP considers alternatives. These alternatives should provide solutions to these problems, such as the back-up emergency generators at the GSA Telework Centers. If this contingency becomes part of your

Appendices

agencies COOP then the Department should investigate and establish agreements with the GSA telework centers now, to ensure that space is available for your agency.

Locations for Telework

Telework locations are also important considerations when evaluating a telework arrangement. The most common two options are listed below along with some thoughts to consider regarding each alternative.

Employee's home-working in a space specifically set aside as an office or other appropriate area in the employee's residence where the employee can perform official work duties. Some considerations may include:

☐ Ensure dependent care arrangements are maintained and do not interfere with the home office.

☐ Work-at-home telework may increase an employees home utility costs. (The Department assumes no responsibility for any operational costs associated with the employees' home residence, including home maintenance, insurance, or utilities.) However, these costs are usually offset by the savings the employee realizes by reducing the cost of their weekly commute to the traditional worksite, reduced lunch money and clothing.

Tips

Government equipment lent to the employee for the purposes of telework are for Official Government Business only. (Maintenance of government owned equipment may require access by approved repairers to the employee's home or the teleworker may have to transport the equipment to the traditional worksite for repairs.)

Satellite facility-working from a telework center or an office near the employee's home, in space owned or leased by one or more agencies. Satellite center employees work there primarily because it is close to their home, not necessarily because they belong to the same work unit. Some considerations for a telework center include:

☐ Onsite technical support and full resources

☐ Telework centers generally provide more traditional work structure

☐ Maintains a clear delineation of work and home life

There is usually a monthly/yearly cost associated with use of a telework center which the Agency will have to agree to cover.

Responsiblities

Work Agreements:

Each employee makes an initial request for telework using the DOJ Flexible Work Option Request form. Employees should consider the following when making telework requests:

☐ Look beyond the benefits to yourself; explain to your supervisor how it will positively benefit your organization.

☐ Start off small by suggesting a day or two a week.

☐ Be willing to be held accountable and self-policing. If you are not self-motivated, offsite work may not suit you.

☐ Create a track record of being reliable and producing quality work.

☐ Maintain a list of your accomplishments. (Particularly those that indicate an ability to work in a more isolated environment.)

☐ Consider the possible effects on your coworkers and clients. Your offsite work should not impose on others by making their work more difficult.

Supervisors will: *(Must Do)*

☐ Review and approve/disapprove employee requests to telecommute;

☐ Evaluate distribution of assignments to ensure equitable distribution of workload; for all workers, in and out of the office.

☐ Develop and amend performance work plans as needed for work performed away from the primary official duty station;

☐ Assign appropriate work to be performed at the alternate duty station and verify that the teleworker has the information and equipment necessary to perform the work independently;

☐ Ensure that work-related documents in both hard copy and electronic form have been adequately secured within the remote work site; and

☐ Periodically evaluate the efficacy of the telework arrangement.

To help teleworkers reduce the feelings of isolation, supervisors should ensure efforts are made to include teleworkers as part of the team.

Plan meetings for days when all teleworkers are scheduled to be in the traditional office.

Teleworkers should be considered equally for the selection of assignments, performance reviews, or any other employer/employee matter.

Supervisors must approve changes in work schedules on telework days and on flexitime schedules in advance to ensure any liability for premium or overtime pay.

Work Schedules:

Work away from the office will vary depending upon the individual arrangements between employees and their supervisors. However, for on-going programs, each telework agreement should provide for a minimum number of days in the office, because:

☐ This will ensure that the employee is available for occasional face-to-face meetings, access to facilities, etc.

Appendices

- Successful programs have shown employees need to spend at least some time in the office to minimize isolation and communication problems, facilitate integration of the employee with those in the office, and to ease supervisor's adjustment.

These hours can parallel the hours in the traditional worksite or be specific to the alternative worksite. However, work schedules must adhere to provisions of existing regulations, government-wide policy and applicable bargaining agreements.

Position Descriptions:

Changes to position descriptions normally should not be required, unless the telework arrangement changes the actual position duties or the position description is not up-to-date. Supervisors should ensure that outdated or nonessential functions are removed and include any minor modifications to supervisory controls or work environment factors.

Performance Management:

- An employee must have a proven or expected (for new employees), performance rating of "fully successful" or equivalent, to be eligible for participation, and for ongoing participation, in the telework program.
- Teleworkers' performance should be monitored in the same manner as all employees' at the traditional worksite. The performance standards should be based on a results-oriented approach and should describe the quantity and quality of expected work products and the method of evaluation.
- Teleworkers are required to complete all assigned work, consistent with the approach adopted for all other employees in the work group, and according to standards and guidelines in the employee's performance plan.

Time, Attendance and Pay

Hours of Duty:

Employees may work standard, flexible, or compressed schedules, depending upon the agreement between the employee and the supervisor.

- The supervisor and the employee select the work-at-home day(s) together.
- There are no limits on the number of telework days vs. in-office days per week; although, it is normally recommended that no more than three work-at-home days per week be allowed.
- Supervisors do have the discretion to allow more than three telework days per week to meet the Department's operational requirements.
- Completely unstructured arrangements where employees work at home at will are not permitted.

☐ Components should adopt a flexible approach in developing optimum arrangements for these employees. Likewise, managers reserve the right to require employees to report to the traditional worksite on scheduled telework days, based on operational requirements.

Leave:

The policies for requesting annual leave, sick leave, or leave without pay remain unchanged. The employee is responsible for requesting leave in advance from the supervisor and keeping the timekeeper informed of leave usage.

Certification and Control of Time and Attendance:

Proper monitoring and certification of employee work time is critical to the success of the program. Supervisors must report time and attendance to ensure that employees are paid only for work performed and that absences from scheduled tours of duty are accounted for correctly.

Administrative Leave, Dismissals and Emergency Closings:

Remember: Although a variety of circumstances may affect individual situations, the principles governing administrative leave, dismissals, and closings remain unchanged. The ability to conduct work, whether at home or at the office, determines when an employee may be excused from duty. For example, if the employee is working at home, and the main office closes, normally the teleworker will continue working at home. However there are some circumstances where this may not be true.

In a situation where an employee's electricity fails while working at home, the supervisor should determine the appropriate action on a case-by-case basis. The supervisor may:

☐ Require the employee to report for work at the traditional worksite

☐ Grant administrative leave: particularly if the government has shutdown due to inclement weather.

☐ Offer the teleworker the option to take leave, compensatory time off or credit hours

☐ When an employee knows in advance of a situation that would preclude working at home, either time in the office or leave should be scheduled.

Working during emergency closures

Employees who telework from home or from an alternative workplace are an invaluable resource to employers for keeping an agency operational during a time of emergency. Therefore, agencies may wish to modify their current policies concerning emergency situations to require telework employees to continue to work at their alternative worksites when the agency is closed. Teleworkers can be required to work during emergency closures even if that day is not a regular telework day or a day with specific approval for situational/episodic telework. If an agency chooses to require an employee to telework during emergency closures either on his or her regular telework day, or on any day when the agency is closed by an emergency, the agency should include this

Appendices

requirement as part of the employee's written telework agreement. On a case-by-case basis, an agency may excuse a telework employee from duty during an emergency if the emergency adversely affects the telework site, if the teleworker is unable to access the alternative telework site (telework center), if the teleworker faces a personal hardship (e.g. child care issues, the inability of telework center teleworkers to get to the centers, etc.) that prevent him or her from working successfully, or if the teleworker's duties are such that he or she cannot continue to work without contact with the regular worksite. Agency management officials are reminded that they should consult with their employees' unions before implementing new, or revised, telework policies.

Fair Labor Standards Act (FLSA):

The existing rules in title 5 U.S.C. and the FLSA governing overtime also apply to telework.

Overtime is time worked at official duties in excess of the scheduled tour of duty that is ordered and approved by the supervisor in advance of that work.

It is the responsibility of the supervisor to regulate and control the use of overtime.

Employees are responsible for requesting, in advance, approval to work in excess of their normal hours of duty. This is particularly important when employees are working at a remote site without direct supervisory oversight.

Managers must ensure that only the work for which it intends to make payment is performed. Since the supervisor is not on the scene, FLSA overtime (or potential liability for FLSA overtime) could be hard to control if clear directions are not provided to participating employees.

Non-exempt telecworkers who work in excess of the hours approved by managers to receive compensation should be removed from the program.

Supervisors should ensure that the employee's work agreement includes a prohibition to working overtime that has not been approved in advance by the supervisor.

Additionally, if employees request supervisory approval first and the work schedule is appropriate given the nature of the work being performed and the level of interaction with the office that is required, employees can extend their work hours to accrue religious compensatory time. Employees must also fulfill all the requirements for eligibility for religious compensatory time.

Other Pay Issues

Duty station:

For pay purposes, the "official duty station" is the employee's Federal office, also referred to as the "traditional worksite".

Special salary rates:

The employee's official duty station serves as the basis for determining special salary rates.

Premium pay:

The normal rules apply for night differentials, and Sunday and holiday pay whether work is accomplished at the conventional or alternate worksite. Official work schedules determine the entitlement to premium pay.

Facilities Issues

Home office space:

Teleworkers should have a designated workspace or work station for performance of their work-at-home duties. Requirements will vary depending on the nature of the work and the equipment needed to perform the work. At a minimum, an employee should be able to easily communicate by telephone with the supervisor during the work-at-home day.

Each participating employee should review the Safety Checklist, which is included as an attachment to the Department's Telework Agreement form, to ensure that the home is safe according to Federal Occupational Safety and Health standards.

- ☐ Employees are responsible for ensuring that their homes comply with these health and safety requirements.
- ☐ Home offices must be clean and free of obstructions.
- ☐ The home must be in compliance with all building codes and free of hazardous materials.

A supervisor may deny an employee the opportunity to participate or may rescind a telework agreement based on safety problems in the home or suspected hazardous materials in the home. The supervisor may also inspect the home office for compliance with safety requirements when deemed appropriate. Inspections will be by appointment only.

The Department does not normally pay home utility costs associated with working at home. Potential savings to the employee resulting from reduced commuting, meals, etc., should offset any incidental increase in utility expenses. Exceptions apply only where the personal expense directly benefits the government, e.g., business-related long distance calls on the employee's personal phone.

GSA-Sponsored Telework Center Workstations:

The component leases a workstation, directly with the Telework center in question, for the employee's use. The employee should visit the Telework center in question, obtain the necessary forms for leasing a workstation and information on the associated costs, and follow component procedures for requesting lease of a Telework center workstation. The Telework Center Director

Appendices

can provide tours of the center, advise employees on the process for obtaining a workstation, and actively assist in doing so.

Telecommunications and Equipment

> Components must identify tools the employee will need while working at the alternative workplace and ensure that the participating employee has access to the necessary reference sources and other materials.
>
> *Remember*

Each organization must establish its own policy on purchase and installation of equipment.

Some organizations may agree to purchase or install equipment, while others, due to budget constraints or other management reasons, may choose not to.

Organizations may make this decision on a case-by-case basis considering such factors as the nature of the work, availability of existing equipment, etc.

In some instances, participation in the program may be contingent on equipment costs or the telecommuter supplying their own, compatible equipment, if equipment is needed to perform the job.

Transfer of computers, printers, modems and other data processing equipment from the office to the home residence and back is determined by the organization. Normally, organizations will make it the responsibility of the individual.

Telephones: For official government business only and specific to telework, Federal agencies may use appropriated funds to pay for telephone installation and basic service in private residences.

Organizations may also pay for the use of the employee's personal phone for business related long-distance phone calls. Current GSA regulations (41 CFR, 101-7i) allow for reimbursement of expenses incurred as a result of official duties on SF-1164, including telephone call expenses approved by the Department.

Computers, government-owned equipment, etc.: Government-owned property, including computers and other telecommunications equipment, may be removed from the Department and used by employees in their private residences provided the equipment is used only for official business. The government must retain ownership and control of hardware, software, and data. In these situations, the government is responsible for maintenance, repair, and replacement of such equipment. The employee must notify his/her supervisor immediately following a malfunction of Government-owned equipment. If repairs are extensive, the employee may be asked to report to the main office until equipment is usable.

Note: If government loaned equipment is unsecured and consequently damaged by non-employees (for example, dependents of the employee) employees may be held liable for the repair or replacement of the equipment, software, etc., to the same extent they are presently held to when loaned equipment is damaged due to their negligence.

Computer Security

Supervisors must ensure that the designated workspace or workstation of the employee has adequate physical or environmental security measures in place to protect the equipment from being accessed by unauthorized individuals.

Only hardware/software equipment procured by the Federal government and authorized by an approving official for the alternate work site should be installed.

Under no circumstances should employees be allowed to add non-government owned or unauthorized hardware or software, such as bulletin board software, to a government issued homework station.

Securing the alternate worksite should include having the employee specifically identify the proposed work area and certify in writing the security measures that will be used. (A checklist, similar to the one being used to certify the safety of the work area may be useful for this purpose).

Examples of measures that may be acceptable, depending upon the information, include denying children access to the work area or securing the work area by locking it when it is not in use.

Components must ensure adequate property management procedures for their property, whether owned or leased.

Program officials and/or teleworkers should ensure that anyone servicing the alternative work site equipment is authorized to do so.

Dial-up telecommunication access to government computers presents special security concerns.

A combination of physical controls, unique user identifiers, passwords, terminal identifiers, access control software, and strict adherence to security procedures is required to protect the information from unauthorized access. This is available through DOJ-supplied software which can be installed on the computer used at the alternate work location.

Ensure that personal IDs, passwords, access codes, etc., that are assigned are accounted for and maintained properly.

If your organization is not already using these types of safeguards, and does not know how to ensure computer security from an alternate work site, contact the Security and Emergency Planning

Appendices

Staff and/or the Information Management and Security Staff in the Justice Management Division for guidance.

Be aware that telephones represent security vulnerability because conversations can be easily intercepted. The normal non-secure telephone cannot be used to discuss classified information.

Teleworkers must comply with component security procedures to protect government information stored on magnetic media of workplace computers when the computers are repaired or serviced.

- ☐ Teleworkers should not rely on software deletion commands such as remove, delete or erase, to fully remove files from the computer.
- ☐ Even though information may appear to be deleted, there is a possibility that it may be retrieved.
- ☐ Where the hard disk of a workplace computer is inoperable, arrangements must be made to remove sensitive information from the hard disk prior to having the computer serviced.

Privacy Act, Sensitive or Classified Data

Decisions regarding the proper use and handling of sensitive data, as well as records subject to the Privacy Act, are delegated to individual supervisors who permit employees to work at home. Offsite access to sensitive data may be permitted provided that the security for such access is adequate.

Care must be taken to ensure that records subject to the Privacy Act and sensitive non-classified data are not disclosed to anyone except to those who are authorized access to such information in order to perform their duties.

Organizations allowing employees to access records subject to Privacy Act from a remote work site must maintain appropriate administrative, technical, and physical safeguards to ensure the security and confidentiality of the records.

Other Issues

Dependent Care

Generally, telework will not significantly reduce dependent care costs. Young children or a loved one with special needs create too many distractions for the employee working at home. Telework is not intended to serve as a substitute for dependent care. However, telework may reduce dependent care costs by reducing the number of hours of care necessary due to time saved commuting. In some cases, it could eliminate the need for before or after school daycare.

Remember

The opportunity to participate in the program is offered only with the understanding that it is the responsibility of the employee to ensure that a proper work environment is maintained (e.g., dependent care arrangements are made so as to not interfere with the work, personal disruptions such as non-business telephone calls and visitors are kept to a minimum, etc.). The employee and his/her family should understand that the home office is just that, a space set-aside for the employee to work. Family responsibilities must not interfere (to the extent they are controllable) with work time at home.

Labor-management relations

Federal employee unions have a right to negotiate on programs that affect bargaining unit employees' conditions of employment. This right extends to telework. The Office of Personnel Management has consulted on telework with the national offices of Federal employee unions and the Department has fulfilled consultation requirements with the American Federation of Government Employees (AFGE). Each organization that wishes to participate in the DOJ Telework Program should refer to the terms of their negotiated agreement or coordinate with their Union to negotiate an agreement.

Training

Supervisors and employers participating in a Telework Program are encouraged to undertake training in telework, as experience shows that the most successful telework arrangements include initial training for both supervisors and employees.

For instance, DOJ has developed a special Manager's Page specifically designed to assist managers. There is a decision tool kit, a manager's tips section and video clips all designed to help the managers successfully negotiate telework and other work place flexibility programs. This site is found at http://www.usdoj.gov/jmd/ps/wlmanagers.html

There is also a wealth of information designed to assist employees with telework and other worklife issues, start with information on the main page and move on from there: http://www.usdoj.gov/jmd/ps/wlbasics.html

For more information on telework training go to: *http://www.usalearning.gov/USALearning/* UAS Learning is the official learning and development site for the Federal government. They have developed a training package for employees and managers to assist in making telework a success.

Appendix 2

Federal Management Regulation; Guidelines for Alternative Workplace Arrangements

Office of Government-wide Policy (MP), General Services Administration [FMR Bulletin 2006–B3]

1. What is the purpose of this bulletin? This bulletin establishes guidelines for implementing and operating alternative workplace arrangements (AWA). These policies are designed to assist agencies in the design and operation of AWA programs as well as to resolve AWA issues commonly faced by agencies.

2. What is the effective date of this bulletin? This bulletin is effective March 17, 2006.

3. When does this bulletin expire? This bulletin will remain in effect indefinitely until specifically cancelled.

4. What are the terms and definitions? Following are terms and definitions used in and for the purposes of this bulletin:

a. Telework and telecommuting are used interchangeably and are defined as the act of performing all or a portion of work functions at an alternative worksite, such as working from home or a telework center, under circumstances that reduce or eliminate the employee's commute. To be considered telework, it must occur at least one day per week on a regular and recurring basis and does not include (1) situational telework (unscheduled, project-oriented, nonrecurring, and/or irregular telework and/or any teleworking that occurs less frequently than once a week on a recurring basis) or (2) full-time mobile work arrangements.

b. AWA includes telecommuting, hoteling, virtual offices, telework centers, hot desking, and other distributed workplace arrangements.

c. Telework center: A facility that (1) provides workstations and other office facilities/services that are utilized (typically on a fee for use/service basis) by employees from several organizations and (2) is used as a geographically convenient alternative worksite for its users.

d. Excess personal property/ equipment: Excess personal property is any personal property that is no longer required by the holding agency for the discharge of its responsibilities.

e. Virtual office or virtual workplace:

A work environment in which employees work cooperatively from different locations using a computer network (in lieu of a single building or other single physical location). As opposed to a single location site (facility) where workers are housed, the virtual office is typically a collaborative communications medium, such as a computer network, where workers gather electronically to collaborate and/or carry out other work activities. The actual physical locations of the employees working in a virtual office can be temporary or permanent and can be nearly anywhere, such as their homes, satellite offices, hotel rooms, corporate offices (shared work space), airports, airplanes, or automobiles.

f. Hoteling: An AWA in which (1) employees work in one facility (facility A) part of the time and at one or more alternative worksites the rest of the time and (2) when working in facility A, these employees use non-dedicated, non-permanent workspaces assigned for use by reservation on an as-needed basis.

g. Hot desking (also known as free address or touchdown workstations): An AWA in which (1) employees work in one facility (facility A) part of the time and at one or more alternative worksites the rest of the time and (2) when working in facility A, these employees use non-dedicated, non-permanent workspaces assigned on a first come, first served basis.

5. What is the background? a. 40 U.S.C. § 587(c)(3), (Pub. L. 104–208, div. A, title I, § 101(f), title IV,

§ 407(a), (September 30, 1996)), as revised, restated and recodified without substantive change by Pub. L. 107–217, August 21, 2002, authorizes GSA to provide guidance, assistance, and oversight, as needed, regarding planning, establishment and operation of AWA.

b. In accordance with 40 U.S.C. § 587(c)(2), (Pub. L. 104–208, div. A, title I, § 101(f), title IV, § 407(a), (September 30, 1996)), as revised, restated, and recodified without substantive change, by Pub. L. 107–217 (August 21, 2002), when considering whether to acquire any space, quarters, buildings, or other facilities for use by employees of any Executive agency, the head of that agency shall consider whether the need for the facilities can be met using AWA.

c. In accordance with section 359 of Public Law 106–346, effective October 23, 2000, each Executive agency must establish a policy under which eligible employees of the agency may participate in telecommuting to the maximum extent possible without diminished employee performance.

d. Guidance and policy from the Office of Personnel Management (February 9, 2001), http://www.telework.gov/twlaws.asp, as reflected in 41 CFR. § 102–74.590, instructs Federal agencies as follows: Many of you already have telecommuting policies, but this does not necessarily mean

Appendices

you are in compliance with the new law. The purpose of the law is to require that each agency take a fresh look at the barriers that currently inhibit the use of this flexibility, act to remove them and increase actual participation. The law recognizes that not all positions are appropriate for telecommuting; therefore, each agency must identify positions that are appropriate in a manner that focuses on broad objective criteria. Once an agency has established eligibility criteria, subject to any applicable agency policies or bargaining obligations, employees who meet them and want to participate must be allowed that opportunity if they are satisfactory performers. e. 40 U.S.C. § 587(d)(2), Public Law 105–277, div. A, § 101(h), title VI, § 630, October 21, 1998, as revised, restated and recodified without substantive change by Public Law 107–217, August 21, 2002, requires that each of the following departments and agencies, in each fiscal year, must make at least $50,000 available from amounts provided for salaries and expenses to pay telework center program user fees: 13846 Federal Register / Vol. 71, No. 52 / Friday, March 17, 2006 / Notices

(1) Department of Agriculture,

(2) Department of Commerce,

(3) Department of Defense,

(4) Department of Education,

(5) Department of Energy,

(6) Department of Health and Human Services,

(7) Department of Housing and Urban Development,

(8) Department of the Interior,

(9) Department of Justice,

(10) Department of Labor,

(11) Department of State,

(12) Department of Transportation,

(13) Department of the Treasury,

(14) Department of Veterans Affairs,

(15) Environmental Protection Agency,

(16) General Services Administration,

(17) Office of Personnel Management,

(18) Small Business Administration,

(19) Social Security Administration,

and

(20) United States Postal Service.

6. Who should we contact for further information regarding locating Federal facilities in rural areas? General Services Administration, Office of Governmentwide Policy, Regulations Management Division, Attn: Stanley C. Langfeld, 1800 F Street, NW., Washington, DC 20405. Telephone Number: (202) 501–1737. E-mail Address: stanley.langfeld@gsa.gov.

Guidelines for Alternative Workplace Arrangements (AWA)

I. Can agencies provide workplace equipment for use at alternative worksites such as employee residences or telework centers? Yes. Agencies may provide/procure either new or excess equipment for alternative worksites as long as it is clear that the equipment continues to belong to the Government and there is an audit trail indicating the location of the equipment. Regarding telecommunications equipment and services that agencies provide to and/or purchase for employees working in home-based or other alternative workplace arrangements (AWA), the following apply:

a. In accordance with Public Law 104–52, section 620; 31 U.S.C. § 1348 note, agencies may use appropriated funds to install telephone lines and necessary equipment, and to pay monthly charges, in any private residence of an employee who has been authorized to work at home in accordance with guidelines issued by the Office of Personnel Management. The head of the department, division, bureau, or office must certify that adequate safeguards against private misuse exist, and that the service is necessary for direct support of the agency's mission.

b. This authority includes facsimile machines, internet services, broadband access, e-mail services, voice over IP equipment and services, desktop videoconference equipment and services, and, in general, any other telecommunications equipment and services the agency deems needed by individuals working in home-based AWA.

c. Based on the same authority used for installing telecommunications equipment for a government employee in a government contractor's office, agencies also are authorized to provide/ procure the telecommunications equipment/services described in paragraph b, above, for employees in non-home-based AWA (such as telework centers).

II. Can agencies provide teleworkers with underutilized equipment (for use in their alternative worksites) before it is declared excess? Yes. Agencies may provide underutilized computers or other equipment for use by teleworkers or for use in other AWA situations. In accordance with 41

Appendices

CFR §§ 102–36.30 and 102–36.35, even though equipment may no longer be used for its original purpose, employee, or location, the agency must determine if the equipment can serve other agency uses, such as in alternative worksites. The equipment does not officially become excess until the agency determines that it cannot be used in main or alternative worksites.

III. Once declared excess by one agency, can computer and/or other equipment be acquired for use by another agency for its telework or other alternative worksite program? Yes. When items are no longer needed by an agency, they are reported to GSA as excess in accordance with 41 CFR part 102–36, Disposition of Excess Personal Property, for possible transfer to other Federal agencies. To learn more about the transfer of excess personal property between Federal agencies, visit About Excess Transfers, on GSA's Property Disposal website.

IV. What help desk and/or other technical support services, if any, can agencies provide to and/or purchase for employees working in home-based telework or other alternative work arrangements?

Agencies may provide or purchase help desk and/or other technical support to employees working in any approved AWA, provided the agency deems the support necessary for successful accomplishment of officially assigned work. Such support services may be provided onsite at the employee's alternative worksite, via telecommunication services such as remote control, at a service site conveniently located to the alternative worksite, at the employing organization's local facility, or using other reasonable means/locations that minimize disruption of the workflow.

V. Can agencies provide/procure office furnishing (e.g., desks, chairs) for alternative worksites? Yes. As with computers and equipment, agencies may provide their own new or used furniture or excess furniture from another agency for alternative worksites, as long as it is clear that the furniture continues to belong to the Government and there is an audit trail indicating the location of the furniture.

VI. Can agencies pay the utility costs for alternative worksites?

The answer depends on the type of alternative worksite. For residential (home-based) alternative worksites, the answer is no. A GAO decision concluded that, absent specific legislative authority, an agency may not use appropriated funds for the reimbursement of employees for incremental utility costs for heating, air conditioning, lighting, and the operation of government-furnished data processing equipment associated with the residential AWA (B–225159, June 19, 1989). For alternative worksites contractually procured by the agency (e.g., telework centers), the agency may pay utility costs associated with employee usage of the site, as long as such expenses are provided for in the contract between the agency and the provider of the site. Regarding alternative worksite arrangements not covered by the latter, the agency may not pay utility costs.

VII. Can agencies require employees to sign a safety checklist to participate in an alternative workplace arrangement? What impact does such a checklist have regarding the Federal Employees' Compensation Act? The answer depends upon the intended use of the checklist. If the checklist is used solely for program purposes, such as acquainting the teleworker with workplace safety, then the agency may require employees to sign such a checklist to participate in the program.

On the other hand, if the checklist is intended to have legal standing for safety and/or liability purposes, then the answer is no. In accordance with Federal Employees' Compensation Act (FECA) Bulletin 98–9 (1998), in providing guidance for determining whether employees injured while working at alternative worksites meet the "performance of duty" criterion for coverage under FECA, employees who are directly engaged in performing the duties of their jobs are covered by FECA, regardless of whether the work is performed on the agency's premises or at an alternative worksite. There is no statement (such as a safety checklist) that can be signed by the employee to negate this coverage.

VIII. Can agencies allow employees to pay for their own alternative workspace? Can agencies establish cost sharing arrangements in which the agency and the employee share the costs for alternative worksite equipment, facilities, and/or services used by the employee?

In cases in which the agency requires an employee to telework or otherwise utilize an alternative worksite, allowing or requiring an employee to pay for or share the costs for the alternative workspace would be an illegal augmentation of the agency's appropriation.

If the agency is not ordering the employee to telework or otherwise utilize an alternative worksite but is, instead, merely allowing the employee to do so, the agency may allow or require the employee to pay for or share the costs for using the alternative space.

Augmentation is a concept of appropriations law that is derived from statute, specifically 31 U.S.C. § 3302(b) (miscellaneous receipts rule) and 31 U.S.C. § 1301(a) (restricting the use of appropriated funds to their intended purposes). The Government Accountability Office has held that an agency may not augment its appropriations from outside sources without specific statutory authority. The concept is related to the separation of powers doctrine. When Congress makes an appropriation, it is also establishing an authorized program level. It is, in effect, telling the agency that it cannot operate beyond the level that it can finance under its appropriation. The objective of the rule against augmentation of appropriations is to prevent a government agency from undercutting the Congressional power of the purse by exceeding the amount Congress has appropriated for that activity.

IX. Can agencies pay taxes charged for residential telephone lines and/or related equipment that is used for officially sanctioned telework purposes? No. The providers of residential telephone lines, services, and/or related telecommunications equipment/services typically charge Federal and

Appendices

State taxes for the acquisition/use of these items. Federal agencies are exempt from Federal taxes and, depending on State tax law, from State taxes as well. Accordingly, agencies are not authorized to pay Federal or, in some cases, State taxes for equipment or services used by their teleworkers.

X. Can agencies authorize teleworkers to make personal use of the alternative worksite equipment provided by the agency? Yes. The head of each agency has the authority to set personal use policies. In accordance with GSA guidance set forth in "Recommended Executive Branch Model Policy/Guidance On Limited Personal Use Of Government Office Equipment Including Information Technology," http://www.cio.gov/ documents/peruselmodellmayl1999.pdf, agencies can authorize teleworkers limited personal use of alternative worksite equipment. Limited personal use of the government office equipment by employees during non-work time is considered to be an "authorized use" of Government property. Authority for this policy is found at 5 U.S.C. § 301, which provides that the head of an executive department or military department may prescribe regulations for the use of its property, and Executive Order 13011 of July 16, 1996, Federal Information Technology, section 3(1), which requires the Chief Information Officers Council to develop recommendations for Federal information technology management policy, procedures, and standards. For more info on this topic, visit the following Web site: http:// www.estrategy.gov/documents/43.pdf.

XI. Who is responsible for the relocation and re-setup of alternative worksite workstations and equipment when an employee relocates? If the relocation of an employee is required by the agency, then the agency is fully responsible for the relocation and re-setup of any associated alternative worksite workstation and/or equipment. If the employee relocates on her/his own accord, then the determination of responsibility for the relocation and re-setup of alternative worksite workstations and equipment (especially agency-owned workstations and equipment) is within the discretion of the agency. When establishing AWA programs, it is the agency's responsibility to establish adequate and equitable policies to cover this issue.

XII. Must the head of an Executive agency consider whether needs can be met using alternative workplace arrangements in considering whether to acquire space, quarters, buildings, or other facilities for use by employees? Yes. In considering whether to acquire space, quarters, buildings, or other facilities for use by employees, 40 U.S.C. § 587(c)(2) requires the head of an Executive agency to consider whether needs can be met using AWA.

XIII. What factors should an Executive agency head consider in considering whether the agency's needs can be met using alternative workplace arrangements? Executive agency heads should consider as many of the following factors as are relevant to the agency's circumstances:

a. Facility performance and space utilization efficiency/effectiveness;

b. Allocation/utilization/flexibility of space to meet diverse/changing organizational needs;

c. Workspace quality factors, quality of worklife;

d. Individual/organizational performance;

e. Technology utilization and return on investment;

f. Reduced/saved facility costs per person;

g. Reduced/avoided other expenses;

h. Increased/earned revenue;

i. Workplace/space flexibility to accommodate/meet diverse/changing uses, configurations, staff, and/or other organizational needs; and

j. Environmental impact, sustainability.

XIV. Should the head of the Executive agency document the result of the agency's consideration of whether to acquire space, quarters, buildings, or other facilities for use by employees? Yes. Documenting the relevant considerations will help the agency make more informed decisions about its immediate space needs and will provide a reference for future agency space considerations. Through early planning, the agency may be able to shorten and simplify the space acquisition process and acquire the necessary space at the most reasonable cost to the Government.

XV. Do space per person standards apply in an alternative worksite environment? No. The Government no longer maintains space per person requirements. Under current GSA space planning guidance, space allocation should be based on organizational needs. When feasible, AWA can accommodate those needs as well as reduce overall agency space requirements. This is the essence of the requirement in 40 U.S.C. § 587(c)(2): use AWA in lieu of new space acquisition to meet agency space needs in a more cost effective and/or otherwise beneficial manner.

APPENDIX 3

Information Technology and Telecommunications Guidelines for Federal Telework and Other Alternative Workplace Arrangement Programs General Services Administration

Guidelines for implementing and operating telework and other alternative workplace arrangement (AWA) programs through the efficient and effective use of information technology and telecommunications. These policies are designed to assist agencies in the implementation and expansion of Federal alternative workplace arrangement programs.

Definitions: Following are terms and definitions used:

a. **Agency Worksite**—An agency worksite is the post of duty to which an employee would report if not teleworking.

b. **Alternative Worksite**—An alternative work location used by teleworkers while teleworking.

c. **Broadband**—Broadband is a term that commonly and loosely refers to high speed data transmission service. When such service is used for connections to the internet, the Federal Communications Commission (FCC) defines two types of connections: (1) high-speed lines that deliver services at speeds exceeding 200 kilobits per second (kbps) in at least one direction, and (2) advanced services lines that deliver services at speeds exceeding 200 kbps in both directions (see FCC News Release entitled "Federal Communications Commission Releases Data On High-Speed Services for Internet Access, High-Speed Connections to the Internet Increased by 33 percent in 2005," dated July 26, 2006, http://hraunfoss.fcc.gov/edocs_public/ attachmatch/DOC-266593A1.doc percent3E).

d. **Dial-up**—Dial-up refers to the use of an analog telephone line for accessing the internet and remotely connecting to and from an alternative worksite to an agency Information Technology (IT) system. Dial-up access uses normal telephone lines for data transmission and generally has a lower data transfer rate as compared to other internet services.

e. **Docking Station**—A docking station is a piece of equipment that is used with a laptop computer to allow for the convenient and quick connection of peripheral and/or telecommunications (internet access, for example) equipment by providing the laptop with additional ports, expansion slots, and bays for various types of peripherals and other connections. Typically, the docking station is continuously located in a given workstation and continuously connected to peripherals and telecommunications access; the laptop is slipped in and out of the docking station, as needed. A docking station also enables use of the laptop to resemble the use and convenience of a desktop computer by enabling the user to operate the laptop with a full size external keyboard, monitor, and/or mouse. Thus, a docking station maintains the flexibility of a laptop while giving it the functionality of a desktop computer.

f. **External Information Systems**— Information systems or components of information systems that are outside of the accreditation boundary established by the organization and for which the organization typically has no direct control over the application of required security controls or the assessment of security control effectiveness. External information systems include, but are not limited to, personally owned information systems (e.g., computers, cellular telephones, or personal digital assistants); privately-owned computing and communications devices resident in commercial or public facilities (e.g., hotels, convention centers or airports); information systems owned or controlled by non-Federal governmental organizations; and Federal information systems that are not owned by, operated by, or under the direct control of the organization.

g. **One Computer Model**—Teleworker use of a single computer, usually a laptop, that is transported to all worksites (typically back and forth between an alternative worksite and the agency worksite). The One Computer Model contrasts with multi-computer situations in which the teleworker has a separate computer for use at each worksite and, typically, each of these computers remains at the worksite and is not transported around.

h. **Remote Access Servers (RAS)**—Remote access servers provide internet and dialup access to the office local area network (LAN). The RAS authenticates the user through a password or stronger mechanism; it then allows the user to access files, printers, or other resources on the LAN. The chief benefit of a RAS is in providing a conveniently packaged comprehensive solution to offsite access needs. Typically, the servers include support for internet-based voice communications, virtual private networks (defined below), and authentication in a package designed to make it easier for administrators to establish and maintain user privileges.

i. **Telework**—Telework is work performed by an employee at an alternative worksite, which reduces or eliminates the employee's commute or travel to the agency worksite. Alternative worksites may include the employee's home, telework center, satellite office, field installation, or other location.

j. **Virtual Private Network (VPN)**—The National Institute of Standards and Technology (NIST) defines VPN as "a logical network that is established, at the application layer of the Open Systems Interconnection (OSI) model, over an existing physical network and typically does not include every node present on the physical network." Further, NIST describes how VPN technology uses the internet as the transport medium and employs security measures to ensure that the communications are private. Although VPN traffic crosses the internet, VPN protection prevents most unauthorized users from reading and/or modifying the traffic (see NIST Special Publication 800–46, Security for Telecommuting and Broadband Communications, http://csrc,nist.gov/ publications/nistpubs/800-46/sp800-46.pdf).

Programs

Basic Equipment Recommendations

a. An agency may provide employees with computer equipment, associated peripheral equipment (e.g., printer, copier, scanner, facsimile), telecommunications, and associated technical support for the implementation and expansion of telework in the Federal government. The agency may provide the level and configuration of these resources that it deems necessary for mission accomplishment. To make this determination, an agency may consider factors such as the teleworker's job requirements, frequency of telework, and other work-related parameters. In addition, the agency is advised to review the 2006 Telework Technology Cost Study, which concluded that the One Computer Model is advantageous from both a value added cost perspective and from a multi-purpose perspective. The 2006 Telework Technology Cost Study is located in the GSA Telework Library at http://www.gsa.gov/telework.

b. An agency may establish a policy that provides that teleworkers utilize their respective alternative worksite equipment and associated technical support for continuity of operations (COOP) purposes. In addition to facilitating COOP responsiveness, this dual-purpose use of telework resources can (1) increase the agency's return on investment for the cost of those resources, as well as (2) reduce agency COOP costs. The NIST Special Publication 800–34, Contingency Planning Guide for Information Technology Systems, provides instructions, recommendations, and considerations for government IT contingency planning (see http://csrc.nist.gov/publications/nistpubs/800-34/sp800-34.pdf), and NIST Special Publication 800–84, Guide to Test, Training, and Exercise Programs for IT Plans and Capabilities, provides additional recommendations and related information(see http://csrc.nist.gov/publications/nistpubs/800-84/SP800-84.pdf.)

c. An agency may provide teleworkers with equipment that is no longer needed for its original purposes, such as when equipment is replaced during a refresh cycle. This strategy can maximize the value of Federal IT investments through the 're-use' or 'repurposing' of equipment to help implement or expand an agency telework program. In accordance with 41 CFR 102–36.30 and 102–36.35, even though equipment may no longer be used for its original purpose, employee, or location, the agency must determine if the equipment can serve other agency uses, such as in alternative worksites. The equipment officially does not become excess until the agency determines that the agency has no further use for the equipment, including use in main or alternative worksites.

Telecommunications and Internet Services

a. Public Law 104–52, section 620, 31 U.S.C. 1348 note, authorizes agencies to use appropriated funds to install telephone lines and necessary equipment, and to pay monthly charges, in any private residence of an employee who has been authorized to work at home in accordance with the guidelines issued by the Office of Personnel Management. The head of the department, division, bureau, or office must certify that adequate safeguards against private misuse exist, and that the service is necessary for direct support of the agency's mission. This authority includes facsimile machines, internet services, broadband access, e-mail services. Voice over Internet Protocol equipment and services, desktop videoconference equipment and services, and, in general, any other telecommunications equipment and services the agency deems needed by individuals working in any authorized alternative worksite.

b. As describe above, agencies are authorized to provide and/or pay for installation and operation of a dedicated voice line for teleworker use at an alternative worksite. Regardless of whether or not, or the extent to which, an agency provides resources for such a line, a dedicated voice line is recommended so that (1) managers, coworkers, clients, and/or other work-related personnel are not prevented from reaching a teleworkers due to the tying up of a teleworker's phone line by online or other data use activity and (2) teleworker do not put themselves at risk by tying up their personal voice line with business activity. Agencies may carry out this recommendation through the use of landlines and/or cell phones.

c. The authorities described above also authorize agencies to pay equipment costs, usage fees, and service charges for all authorized methods of connectivity (e.g., dial-up, high-speed, wireless, satellite) utilized for official business at alternative worksites.

d. Factors such as teleworker job requirements, telecommunications service availability, and quality and cost of service at the alternative worksite should be used to determine teleworker connectivity. Various types of high-speed telecommunication services are available in many areas and not in others. Speed, performance, reliability, and cost are factors to consider when determining how to meet connectivity requirements. In some instances, for example, in which an analog telephone line is the only available connectivity solution, the resulting dial-up access may be sufficient, depending on the teleworker's job requirements. Agency policies should address the equitable provisioning of these resources. It is recommended that agencies implement more than one type of connectivity because of variations in service availability, teleworker job requirements and modes of operation, and other factors that impact the type of connectivity required.

e. Security and connectivity requirements vary according to whether or not a teleworker's job requires interacting with an agency's centralized IT systems. Teleworkers who do not require interaction with an agency's centralized IT systems may be able to telework successfully using only e-mail and telephone contact with the office, without logging into the agency system. For

Appendices

example, a user who teleworks one or two days per week, and whose job consists largely of writing and document preparation, may never need to log in to agency systems from an alternative worksite. Provided that they are not sensitive or do not contain personally identifiable information, documents can be e-mailed back and forth between the agency system and the user's email account. In this scenario, e-mailing a document from an alternative worksite to the agency system does not require the teleworker to interact with the system. In general, there are may firewall implementations that use an electronic mail proxy to allow access to the files on a protected system without having to directly access that system. Alternatively, the teleworker may physically transport the documents on portable storage media. When teleworkers need to access the agency's centralized IT systems, it is necessary, at a minimum, to allow for remote logins from the alternative worksite computer. In this case, strong authentication (at least "two factor authentication") is required to minimize the vulnerabilities in providing external access. This solution is sufficient for teleworkers requiring minimal access to internal resources, such as some types of intranet access. NIST provides detailed guidance on this issue in Special Publication 800–63, its document on electronic authentication, and agencies are advised to review and comply with this guidance (see http://csrc.nist.gov/ publications/nistpubs/800-63/SP800-63V1-0-2.pdf).

Some teleworkers, however, may require more involved access to internal resources. In this case, a more secure solution, such as a VPN, should be used. A VPN can provide a high level of security and convenience for the teleworker. Encryption protects all interaction between the offsite computer and the main office, so that in many ways the user's offsite computer is as secure as one on the main office local network. This approach makes it possible to allow offsite users to operate applications such as scheduling, budget analysis, or other complex systems from the alternative worksite. The tradeoff for a VPN is in cost and complexity of administration. Note also that operating a VPN does not guarantee protection from viruses and e-mail worms. The agency Chief Information Officer (CIO), in conjunction with other agency officials (such as telework and/or human resources management policy providers), should examine job requirements and provide policy, guidance, and appropriate secure system access.

f. Agencies should be aware and take advantage of the potential utility and other benefits of audio teleconference and web conference capabilities for their respective telework programs. These capabilities can be excellent tools to facilitate productivity, agency cost savings (from reduced travel expenses, for example), and other benefits for all employees, in general, and for teleworkers, in particular. Agency telework program planners and implementers should be aware of and utilize the relevant telecommunications products, tools, information, and services that are available in their existing contracts and/or from service providers, such as the GSA Global Account Manager (*http://www.gsa.gov/networkscvs*), or equivalent sources and providers.

Security

a. According to an Office of Management and Budget (OMB) memorandum entitled "Protection of Sensitive Agency Information," dated June 23, 2006, which addresses the lack of physical security controls when information is removed from or accessed from outside the agency location, agencies should implement the NIST checklist for protection of remote information (see http://www.whitehouse.gov/omb/memoranda/fy2006/m06-16.pdf), and:

(1) Encrypt all data on mobile computers and devices that carry agency data, unless the agency determines that the data are nonsensitive;

(2) Allow remote access only with two factor authentication where one of the factors is provided by a device separate from the computer gaining access;

(3) Use a "time-out" function requiring user re-authentication after thirty (30) minutes of inactivity for remote access and mobile devices; and

(4) Log all computer-readable data extracts from databases holding sensitive information and verify that each such extract has been erased within ninety (90) days or that its use is still required.

b. FISMA delegates to NIST the responsibility to develop detailed information security standards and guidance for Federal information systems, with the exception of national security systems.

Agency personnel involved in planning, implementing, and/or operating telework programs should consult the Web site of NIST's Computer Security Resource Center (see *http://csrc.nist.gov*) for up-to-date information and guidance on secure computing. Listed below are key documents that can assist in the implementation of secure telework operations.

(1) Security for Telecommuting an Broadband Communications (NIST Special Publication 800–46 (2002)), assists organizations in addressing telework security issues by providing recommendations on securing a variety of applications, protocols, and network architectures (see http://csrc.nist.gov/publications/nistpubs/800-46/sp800-46.pdf).

(2) Recommended Security Controls for Federal Information Systems (NIST Special Publication 800–53, Rev. 1 (2006)), provides important guidance on security controls selection and specification, including information on Media Protection, Certification, Accreditation, Security Assessments, Identification and Authentication families, updating security controls, and the use of external information systems (see http://csrc.nist.gov/publications/nistpubs/index.html#sp800-53-Rev1).

(3) Information Security Handbook: A Guide for Managers (see http://csrc.nist.gov/publications/nistpubs/#sp800-100).

Appendices

(4) Security Management and guidance (see http://csrc.nist.gov).

c. Agencies should review and comply with applicable controls and guidance, especially sections on portable devices, remote access, and external IT systems set forth in NIST Special Publication 800–53, Rev. 1, when developing telework program implementation guidelines. Listed below are selected controls and guidance from NIST Special Publication 800–53, Rev. 1:

(1) Access Control for Portable and Mobile Devices (e.g., notebook computers, personal digital assistants, cellular telephones, and other computing and communications devices with network connectivity and the capability of periodically operating in different physical locations):

i. Establish usage restrictions and implementation guidance for organization-controlled portable and mobile devices;

ii. Authorize, monitor, and control device access to organizational information systems;

iii. Require that portable and mobile device access to organizational information systems be in accordance with organizational security policies and procedures. Security policies and procedures include device identification and authentication, implementation of mandatory protective software (e.g., malicious code detection, firewall), configuration management, scanning devices for malicious code, updating virus protection software, scanning for critical software updates and patches, conducting primary operating system (and possibly other resident software) integrity checks, and disabling unnecessary hardware (e.g., wireless, infrared).

(2) Remote Access:

i. Authorize, monitor, and control all methods of remote access to the information system. Remote access controls should be applied to all information systems other than public web servers or systems specifically designed for public access;

ii. Restrict access achieved through dial-up connections (e.g., limit dial-up access based upon source of request) or protect against unauthorized connections or subversion of authorized connections (e.g., using VPN technology). NIST Special Publication 800–63 provides guidance on remote electronic authentication;

iii. Employ automated mechanisms to facilitate the monitoring and control of remote access methods;

iv. Use cryptography to protect the confidentiality and integrity of remote access sessions;

v. Control all remote accesses through a limited number of managed access control points; and

vi. Permit remote access for privileged functions only for compelling operational needs and document the rationale for such access in the security plan for the information system.

(3) Use of External Information Systems Control:

i. Establish terms and conditions for authorized individuals to: (A) access the information system from an external information system; and (B) process, store, and/or transmit organization-controlled information using an external information system. Authorized individuals include organizational personnel, contractors, or any other individuals with authorized access to the organizational information system. This control does not apply to the use of external information systems to access organizational information systems and information that are intended for public access (e.g., individuals accessing Federal information through public interfaces to organizational information systems).

ii. Establish terms and conditions for the use of external information systems in accordance with organizational security policies and procedures. The terms and conditions should address, at a minimum: (A) the types of applications that can be accessed on the organizational information system from the external information system; and (B) the maximum Federal Information Processing Standard 199 security category of information that can be processed, stored, and transmitted on the external information system.

iii. Prohibit authorized individuals from using an external information system to access the information system or to process, store, or transmit organization-controlled information except in situations where the organization: (A) Can verify the employment of required security controls on the external system as specified in the organization's information security policy and system security plan; or (B) has approved information system connection or processing agreements with the organizational entity hosting the external information system.

IV. Privacy

Agencies should review the OMB memorandum entitled "Safeguarding Personally Identifiable Information," dated May 22, 2006, and ensure that their respective telework technology infrastructures, practices and procedures are in compliance with that memorandum and the Privacy Act. The OMB memorandum reemphasizes the many responsibilities under law and policy to safeguard sensitive personally identifiable information appropriately. Among other things, the Privacy Act requires each agency to establish: "Rules of conduct for persons involved in the design, development, operation, or maintenance of any system of records, or in maintaining any record, and instruct each such person with respect to such rules and the requirements of [the Privacy Act], including any other rules and procedures adopted pursuant to [the Privacy Act] and the penalties for noncompliance;" [and] "appropriate administrative, technical, and physical safeguards to insure the security and confidentiality of records and to protect against any anticipated threats or hazards to their security or integrity which could result in substantial harm, embarrassment, inconvenience, or unfairness to any individual on whom information is maintained." (5 U.S.C. 552a(e)(9)–(10))

Appendices

V. Training

Teleworkers should receive adequate training on the use of IT systems and applications needed for effective job performance. This should include any specialized training associated with (1) effective use of remote access and other resources needed for working remotely, and (2) security awareness and responsibility. In addition, agencies are encouraged to provide opportunities for teleworkers to practice in a telework situation.

VI. Technical Support

a. Agencies should (1) provide adequate and effective Help Desk support for teleworkers, and (2) require Help Desk personnel to possess the skills, procedures, and resources needed for resolving teleworker issues, such as remote access hardware and software issues.

b. Where feasible and applicable, agencies should provide routine systems maintenance via remote transmission procedures such as transmitting ("pushing") software and system upgrades out to the teleworker's alternative worksite as opposed to requiring the teleworker to bring a computer to the agency worksite for maintenance.

VII. Additional References and Resources

a. Office of Management and Budget (see http://www.whitehouse.gov/omb/memoranda/m03-18.pdf).

b. Government Accountability Office (see http://www.gao.gov).

VIII. Commonly Asked Questions

a. May an employee use his or her own personal computer equipment to conduct official business from an alternative worksite? If so, who is responsible for maintaining an employee's personally-owned equipment that is used for official business?

Yes, provided certain conditions are met, agencies may permit employees to use personally-owned equipment to conduct official business. If an agency permits the use of personally owned equipment, the employee must agree to allow the agency to (1) configure that equipment with the proper hardware and software necessary for secure and effective job performance, and (2) access the equipment, as needed, to verify compliance with agency policy and procedures. Additional conditions that must be met are set forth in NIST Special Publication 800–53, Rev. 1, on page 64, as follows: "The organization prohibits authorized individuals from using an external information system to access the information system or to process, store, or transmit organization-controlled information except in situations where the organization: (i) Can verify the employment of required security controls on the external system as specified in the organization's information security policy and system security plan; or (ii) has approved information system connection or processing agreements with the organizational entity hosting the external information system."

If the agency allows the use of personally-owned equipment for official business, then the telework agreement should clearly identify the employee's and agency's obligations for appropriate operation, repair, and maintenance of the equipment. While agencies are responsible for Government-owned equipment regardless of location, they are not required to be responsible for employee-owned equipment. At their sole discretion, however, agencies may assume responsibility for employee-owned equipment that is used to conduct official business. For example, agencies may authorize Help Desks or other agency personnel or resources to (1) fix a problem with the employee's personally-owned equipment, (2) help the employee fix the problem, or (3) provide, install, and/or upgrade Government-owned software on employee-owned equipment. If an agency permits the use of personally-owned equipment, the employee must agree to allow the agency to configure that equipment with the proper hardware and software including security, communications and applications.

b. Are there policies for "limited personal use" of Government e-mail and internet systems?

Yes. The Office of Management and Budget expects all agencies to establish personal use policies consistent with the recommended guidance developed by the CIO Council in 1999 (see "Personal Use Policies and 'File Sharing' Technology" memorandum at: http://www.whitehouse.gov/omb/ memoranda/fy04/m04-26.html). In addition, NIST Special Publication 800–53, Rev. 1, under the section titled Supervision and Review—Access Control, recommends that agencies supervise and review the activities of users with respect to the enforcement and usage of information system access controls.

According to this guidance, agencies should review audit records (e.g., user activity logs) for inappropriate activities in accordance with organizational procedures and investigate unusual information system-related activities.

c. Are there any other Guidelines for Alternative Workplace Arrangements?

Yes. For additional guidance, see FMR Bulletin, 2006–B3, Guidelines for Alternative Workplace Arrangements, Sections I through XV, dated March 17, 2006.

Appendix 4

Department of Justice Telework Program Agreement

I. Pay, Leave and Travel

a. All pay, special salary rates, leave and travel entitlements will be based on the employee's official duty station.

b. The employee agrees to pay all of the travel expenses to and from the employee's official and alternative duty stations, including return trips to the official duty station for emergency meetings.

c. Employee's timekeeper will have a copy of the employee's telework schedule.

Employee's time and attendance will be recorded as performing official duties at the official duty station, as long as the employee is in the official duty station at least one day per week.

d. Employees must obtain supervisory approval before taking leave in accordance with established office procedures. By signing this form, employee agrees to follow established procedures for requesting and obtaining approval of leave.

e. Employee will continue to work in pay status while working at alternate worksite.

If employee works overtime that has been ordered and approved in advance, he/she will be compensated in accordance with applicable law and regulations.

The employee understands that the supervisor will not accept the results of unapproved overtime work and will act vigorously to discourage it. By signing this form, employee agrees that failing to obtain proper approval for overtime work may result in her/his removal from teleworking or other appropriate action.

f. The employee agrees that he or she will not engage in dependent care or allow personal business or other employment, whether for compensation or not, to interfere with official business during established duty hours for the duration of this agreement. If a need to attend to such other business arises during duty hours, the employee will request leave following the normal procedures.

II. Work Assignments and Performance

a. Employee will meet with the supervisor to receive assignments and to review completed work as necessary or appropriate.

b. Employee will complete all assigned work according to work procedures mutually agreed upon by the employee and the supervisor and according to guidelines and standards stated in the employee's performance plan.

c. Employee may be required to attend meetings, conferences, or training or to otherwise come to the official duty station on days or hours normally scheduled for the alternative work site.

d. Employee's job performance will be evaluated on criteria and milestones derived from past performance, occupational standards, and/or other standards consistent with these guidelines as determined by the supervisor and will be consistent with those of non-teleworking coworkers.

e. Employee's current performance plan contains performance standards covering work completed at the official duty station as well as work completed at the employee's alternate worksite.

f. Employee's most recent performance rating of record must be fully successful or higher.

III. Facilities

a. Employee is required to review the self-certification checklist on home safety for telework. Employee is responsible for ensuring that the home office is clean; free of obstructions or potential safety hazards; in compliance with all buildings codes; and free of hazardous materials. The supervisor may deny the request to participate or may rescind a telework agreement based on safety problems in the home.

b. Provided the employee is given at least 24 hours advance notice, the employee agrees to permit inspections by the Government of the employee's alternate worksite at periodic intervals during the employee's normal working hours to ensure proper maintenance of Government-owned property and worksite conformance with safety standards and other specifications in these guidelines.

c. The Government will not be liable for damages to an employee's personal or real property during the course of performance of official duties or while using

Government equipment in the employee's residence, except to the extent the

Government is held liable by Federal Tort Claims Act claims or claims arising under the Military Personnel and Civilian Employees Claims Act.

Appendices

d. The Government will not be responsible for operating costs, home maintenance, or any other incidental costs (e.g., utilities) whatsoever, associated with the use of the employee's residence. While teleworking, the employee does not relinquish any entitlement to reimbursement for authorized expenses incurred while conducting business for the Government, as provided for by statute and implementing regulations.

IV. Equipment and Support Services

a. If employee borrows Government equipment, employee will protect the Government equipment. Government-owned equipment will be serviced and maintained by the Government. If employee provides own equipment, he/she is responsible for servicing and maintaining it.

V. Injury on the Job

a. Employee is covered under Federal Employee's Compensation Act if injured in the course of actually performing official duties at the official duty station or within the designated space of an alternate worksite.

b. Any accident or injury occurring at the alternate worksite must be brought to the immediate attention of the supervisor. Because an employment-related accident sustained by a teleworking employee will occur outside the premises of the official duty station, the supervisor must investigate all reports immediately following notification.

VI. Security

a. Employee will apply approved safeguards to protect Government/agency records from unauthorized disclosure or damage and will comply with the Privacy Act requirements set forth in the Privacy Act of 1974, P.L. 93-579, codified at section 552a, title 5 U.S.C.

b. Employee will comply with the provisions specified in DOJ Order 2640.2E, Information Technology Security when teleworking in order to protect access to DOJ electronic information and computer systems.

VII. Termination of Agreement

a. Employee may terminate participation in telework at any time. Management has the right to remove the employee from a telework arrangement if the employee's performance declines or if the arrangement fails to support organizational needs; such removal must be accomplished in accord with established administrative procedures and union negotiated agreements.

b. Employee agrees to limit her/his performance of her/his officially assigned duties to her/his official duty station or to agency approved alternative worksites. Failure to comply with this provision may result in loss of pay, termination of the telework arrangement, and/or other appropriate disciplinary action.

Appendix 5

From Work to Telework – Small and Smart Mobile Solutions

From 'To Work' to Telework: Small and Smart Mobile Solutions for Public Servants, A Strategy Paper from Center for Digital Government

Virtual Vocabulary

Hoteling — Use of a single work space in the central office that is shared by several employees who typically work offsite instead of each employee having a separate workspace.

Millennials or Generation Y — Those born from 1982 to the mid-1990s. They have a reputation for being peer-oriented and for seeking instant gratification.

Personal peak time — The time of day or night when an individual is most effective or achieves maximum work productivity.

Smartphone — A mobile phone offering advanced capabilities beyond a typical cell phone, often with PC-like functionality. It typically runs operating system software providing a standardized interface and platform for application developers and advanced features such as e-mail and Internet capabilities.

Telework — A work arrangement in which employees enjoy flexibility in working location and hours, with the daily commute to a central place of work replaced by telecommunication links. Many work from home, while others utilize mobile telecommunications technology to work from coffee shops or myriad other locations.

Virtual Office — A fully functional worksite that is not bound to a specific location but is portable and scalable, connecting employees to the work process in the most advantageous setting, rather than employees having to come to a central office to connect to the work process.

Virtual Worker — Employees who consistently work at home or at a remote location with no designated work space or computer equipment provided at a central office.

Smartphones have already changed the world of work once, allowing users to make and receive calls, send e-mail, check calendars and tasks and use the Internet at a time and place of their choosing. That's only the beginning of the story. For individual users, these small and smart devices are putting the personal back into personal computing. Just as the PC revolution began at the desktop and moved to the laptop, laptops are now giving way to smartphones as the mobile device of choice for generations of workers more accustomed to the possibilities of telework with the flexibility to choose how and where they do their work.

The use of smartphones for conducting business is at a tipping point due to several advancements, including network speed and increased connectivity; device horsepower and better screen resolution; the addition of global positioning software; more multimedia capabilities; availability of more robust applications on the device; Department of Defense-approved encryption; and increased access to the organization's enterprise applications. End users, especially Millennials, are quickly gaining expertise by using smartphones as their mobile interface to work.

Institutionally, smartphones bring unprecedented flexibility to contingency planning and business continuity when physical work places become inaccessible or unavailable. When employees are already familiar with working remotely, they are not sidelined when disaster strikes. Snow days and minor floods no longer mean sitting at home idle, waiting to get into the office. Today's smartphone applications allow users to collaborate.

They can access, edit and file documents and presentations; access enterprise systems; manage IT systems; and support public protection and continuity of operations. Through new mobile applications, they also extend the value of enterprise systems by making mission critical data — public safety, health and human services case management, citizen interaction management and regulatory inspections — available in real time.

"There are a number of agencies that now use telework in their COOP programs and planning," said Eric Kretz, deputy division director for the Federal Emergency Management Agency's National Continuity of Operations Programs (COOP). "Many of the smaller agencies are relying on telework 100 percent for their COOP program, and some of them are well positioned to accomplish it."

Predictions about the impact of smartphones over the next five years are being proven true as smartphones have overtaken laptops in their use as mobile devices for managers and are gaining in use among non-managers. A recent survey found that while access to personal information management (PIM) applications — voice and electronic mail and instant messaging — remains in the lead at 66 percent among Federal teleworkers, use of pocket-sized devices to access backend systems (25 percent), desktop applications (41 percent) and support of continuity of operations (43 percent) is expanding.

Moreover, these changes coincide with political and public attention to environmental sustainability. This new emphasis on technology that supports going green positions smartphones as more than a device for taking calls and checking messages. They are quickly becoming an

Appendices

integral infrastructure supporting mobility that realizes three complementary goals: optimizing productivity by making information available when and where it is needed; equipping employees for mobile working without the extensive infrastructure costs of providing separate and secure network connectivity; and reducing the number and distance of trips for public employees doing their jobs.

Benefits: Why telework?

As mobility increases in popularity, it is transforming government by making it leaner and greener. The drivers for going mobile with smartphone technology are compelling and include cost and time savings, decreasing the government's impact on the environment and a variety of organizational benefits. For example, Arizona embraced the concept so thoroughly that 4,328 employees actively participate in its telework program. Officials estimate that the state's teleworkers annually drive 5.25 million fewer miles, generate 175,000 fewer pounds of air pollution and endure 181,000 fewer hours of stressful driving time. Research finds that by teleworking full time, the average commuter can save more than $2,000 a year on gas.

Government agencies are becoming greener by reducing their office space needs through telework programs. These organizations are implementing hoteling (see page 3's 'Virtual Vocabulary') instead of allocating individual workspaces for mobile workers. The Treasury Department estimates that it saves $1 million annually on rent through its telework program.

This trend also includes the assignment of cell phones only, eliminating landlines for employees who work in the field or from home.

"The greenest building is the one that is never built," said Paul Taylor, chief strategy officer for the Center for Digital Government. "By increasing mobile access to systems and implementing telework programs, government can significantly reduce its office space needs."

Cost savings are also realized through remote access to systems and information by reducing or eliminating trips to government facilities for public servants and citizens. This approach reduces pollution, saves time and lowers gas consumption. Organizations that are going mobile with smartphones are also reducing costs since these devices are less expensive than laptops. Smartphones have other advantages over laptops as well since they serve multiple purposes — connectivity, voice mail and e-mail — and employees are able to carry fewer devices and be productive in places where laptops are impractical, such as on foot.

Less obvious, but equally important, are the positive benefits that telework and mobile access bring to organizations. These benefits include increasing employee productivity, boosting job satisfaction, attracting and retaining talent and increasing employee retention. Arizona found that employees involved in its telework program are more productive on non-commute days.

This increase is due to the elimination of stress that accompanies most employees' commutes — negative impacts to blood pressure, mood, tolerance and increases in the frequency of illness to name a few. Additionally, employees who telework are able to take advantage of their personal peak time. Telework and mobile access also allow governments to attract employees who are not located nearby but can work just as effectively from a remote location. It has the net effect of expanding their options for finding top talent — especially for hard-to-fill positions.

Culture: A changing workforce

As the population adopts and adapts to emerging technologies, so does the public sector workforce. Recent statistics show that more than 71 percent of adults in the United States use the Internet, with nearly 50 percent of their households gaining access via a high-speed broadband connection. This level of usage is transforming government employees into a workforce that demands connectivity and access to information and digital resources, regardless of place or time. While some baby boomers and Gen Xers complain that today's communication technologies are a leash that does not allow them to get far from the office, when surveyed, 91 percent of Federal employees give smartphones high marks for helping them stay organized and remain connected to their job. In fact, they believe it has a positive impact on their professional productivity.[7] The government workforce is aging, and baby boomers — a significant percentage of the current workforce — are quickly heading toward retirement. According to NASCIO, 27 percent of state IT workers are eligible to retire in the next five years.

The significant number of government employees heading toward retirement combined with the next generation of government workers who expect technology to be mobile, intuitive and always on will accelerate the demand for connectivity and access in the near future. For Millennials, multitasking comes naturally, staying connected is not optional and being tied down to one place is unacceptable. These personal habits drive their workplace expectations.

The trend toward flexible work location is growing with government leading the way. Recent statistics show that the Federal sector has an average of about 17 percent of their employees working offsite while the private sector averages around 14 percent. States are embracing teleworking too, with Arizona and Virginia leading the way.

In Maricopa County, Ariz., the number of government virtual workers has reached more than 20 percent, which is higher than the averages for the Federal government and the private sector. The shift toward a more mobile workforce did not occur by accident. It is the result of a 15-year effort that includes a well-documented process, which embraces the concept of mobility as a business strategy, not another trend to try and then abandon when challenges arise.

In Virginia, Gov. Timothy Kaine recently announced an initiative to encourage gubernatorial appointees to telework. The state also released an improved telework policy "directing all state

Appendices

agencies to consider ways to improve and expand agency telework." The Virginia Information Technologies Agency (VITA) is ahead of the curve in implementing their state's policy, with more than 40 percent of their IT workforce teleworking at least one time per week, according to Aneesh Chopra, VITA's secretary of technology.

"The commonwealth is not unlike any other business that implements telework," said Karen Jackson, director of Virginia's Office of Telework Promotion and Broadband Assistance.

"We want to maximize cost savings, increase operational efficiencies, recruit and retain the best employees without regard to geographic boundaries and provide a quality of life for our employees all while maintaining only the highest level of constituent customer service."

Changes in the government workforce go beyond the worker and include the need for supervisors to adjust their management style. Virtual supervisors understand that the best way to judge employee performance is by measuring results, not appearances or the amount of face time they have with an employee. Arizona leaders recommend their supervisors apply this approach to employees whether they are working at or away from the official worksite. Virtual supervisors also understand the need to schedule feedback since spontaneous praise may be less likely to occur when employees are out of sight.

Challenges: Attitudes, policies, funding and security

The adoption of smartphones as the mobile device of choice for public servants requires addressing issues of security, funding and support. It also means overcoming organizational barriers and traditions while matching technology to the culture of public agencies. Early adopters agree that attitudes and ignorance are the biggest barriers when moving forward with a more mobile workforce. Often, organizations are unsure of how to get started, select the right positions and people, manage employees that they cannot see and what success looks like.

Traditional supervisors who focus on adherence to strict work hours and face time with employees must learn new management styles that focus on productivity and outcomes to successfully supervise remote employees. Additionally, government agencies that believe they must treat every employee the same in order to be fair must get past the idea that their telework program has to be for everyone or no one at all.

According to Arizona's Telework Supervisors' Web site, "Offering the opportunity to telework is a management option, not a universal employee benefit."

Sometimes change of this magnitude must come from the top to be embraced. When Virginia CIO Lem Stewart faced challenges implementing a telework program for Virginia's IT agency, he first required his executive staff to telework at least one day a week. He even included himself in this policy, working from home a few days a week. He then expanded the program to middle management, requiring them to do some of their work from home. Stewart said this approach helped his management team become more supportive of the telework program.

The multi-disciplinary nature of telework poses another implementation challenge for agencies desiring to establish a program. Representatives from IT, human resources, security and management are needed to support it. The number of functional areas participating in the program can quickly expand depending on the nature and scope of the desired mobile workforce.

Additionally, a recent study found that about half of the organizations with telework programs lack formal policies to address security and privacy concerns, and comprehensive training programs are needed to ensure smooth operations. To address these issues, Arizona created a Virtual Office Steering Committee consisting of human resources, IT and training experts who address policies and oversight. They also have a well-documented, thorough assessment and training program for everyone involved in the program — employees, supervisors and decision makers.

Another issue government agencies face in the transition to mobile devices is funding. Early adopters encourage organizations to transition to mobile devices as part of their standard equipment refresh program, moving away from traditional desktop computers and landlines to smartphones and other mobile devices. Governments should avoid the temptation to use obsolete devices or cascade older equipment in their telework programs as mobility actually requires a refresh toward modern computing features. While keeping mobile data secure is a top priority for a majority of Federal chief information security officers (CISOs), according to a 2007 Report from Telework Exchange, 94 percent believe teleworkers in an official program are not a data security concern. Instead, Federal CISOs are concerned when employees work from home outside of a formal program — on their own initiative, at night or on weekends. In that scenario, employees are often working in an environment that lacks appropriate data security education, tools and technologies.

In government telework programs such as those in Virginia, Arizona and Portland, Ore., teleworkers use their own equipment and pay for their own broadband when they work at home. These employees often work remotely one or two days per week. While this approach works when it is part of a sanctioned program with strong education, technologically savvy teleworkers and systems with data that is not highly sensitive, the use of personally owned technology to perform government work can be a serious security breach when it is not part of sanctioned program. Often, government employees use personal devices to meet service requirements when access to mobile devices, such as smartphones, are restricted to upper management. This approach is perilous for several reasons, especially when:

Appendices

- ☐ information stored on personal devices is not backed up or stored securely;
- ☐ personal devices do not have adequate and/or up-to-date malware fighting software to prevent the introduction of viruses, Trojan horses, etc., into the government environment;
- ☐ the agency's security software is not installed on personal devices, secure configuration is not in place and standard security practices are not followed;
- ☐ the ability to push out upgrades and up-to-date versions of malware prevention and security software, as well as remotely kill destructive programs are not available;
- ☐ commingling personal and work-related communication on or through a single device may put users and their agencies at risk of violating their respective ethics rules; and
- ☐ the ability to respond appropriately to Freedom of Information Act requests is compromised when government information is stored on personal devices.

Public purpose: Where telework is working

Federal, state and local government agencies are increasingly moving workers out of the office. These successful telework programs share common factors including executive-level support; formal legislation; a well-documented, multi-disciplinary program with education and assessment; written policies; and investments in infrastructure to support telework and drivers, such as the need to reduce congestion and pollution or additional ways to attract and retain talent.

In addition to Arizona and Virginia, the states of California, Georgia and Washington have strong telework programs. Since the early 1990s, California has encouraged every state agency to "review their work operations and establish telework programs in work areas where they have identified telework as both practical and beneficial." Its comprehensive program, outlined on the CA.gov Web site, includes information for scheduling, equipment, software, security, setting up a telework environment and health and safety measures.

Like California, Washington has a well-documented telework program that was established in 2001. Georgia embraced telework in 2002 by launching the "Work Away" telework program to realize the benefits of teleworking and to encourage the state's employers to do the same. This successful program led to passage of a telework tax credit, making Georgia the first state in the nation to offer tax credits for employers with telework programs.

Telework is working at the local level as well, with the Metro Denver area, in Colorado, leading the way. In 2006, it was named one of the best regions for teleworking by Sperling's BestPlaces for its emphasis on sustainability, percentage of high-tech companies and advanced telecommunications infrastructure.

The Denver Regional Council of Governments offers a free telework consulting service for employers in the Denver area. Using a Telework Toolkit, it provides information, materials, expert advice and hands-on assistance to area employers to help them create a customized telework program. The telework program in Portland, Ore., requires a signed agreement and includes home office visits by supervisors and outlines requirements for personal equipment used by teleworkers to perform city work. The City of Austin, Texas, revitalized its telework program in response to declining air quality in the region.

Through FAQs, the program addresses managers' concerns regarding monitoring work and how the program works. From agriculture to veteran's affairs, Federal workers are teleworking.

According to recent surveys of Federal employees, 70 agencies reported having a telework program. Mobile Federal employees report that they save an average of 54 minutes per day using smartphones. Understanding and supporting the benefits of telework, more than half of these Federal agencies consider telework requirements when making IT infrastructure investments. In addition to driving procurement decisions, several Federal agencies, such as the Department of Defense, Department of Health and Human Services and General Services Administration (GSA) report tracking return on investments in telework. Through its Web site, www.telework.gov, GSA and the U.S. Office of Personnel Management share policies and program details and encourage collaboration among Federal telework coordinators.

Tomorrow: What's on the horizon

Imagine a citizen using their smartphone to report a pothole, complete with a photo and GPS location information, via a mobile-friendly government Web site. The information is then transparently routed as a service request to the appropriate field worker's smartphone device. Once the work is done, the service request is marked complete and the citizen is automatically notified and thanked for reporting the problem. Imagine a citizen calling 3-1-1 to report graffiti on public property and assisted by a government employee working from home who has real-time access to systems to enter the service request, which is automatically routed to the right person where its progress can be tracked. Advances in technology and communication infrastructure are bringing these visions closer to reality.

In fact, New York is already soliciting photos in mobile reports from residents who serve as an informal network of eyes and ears in all corners of America's largest city.

Former Arizona Gov. Janet Napolitano imagines a future where services provided in traditional brick and mortar facilities are transitioned to a virtual office environment. State call centers topped her list of functions that will operate virtually in the near future. Given the success of Arizona's current telework program, her vision will soon become a reality.

"Over the next five years, more and more state employees will transition from traditional work spaces to home offices," she said. "Virtual offices save money in office space, shrink the state's carbon footprint, increase employee morale and reduce turnover."

Appendices

Walls are being torn down between enterprise computing and mobile connectivity that will merge the power of applications such as customer relationship management (CRM) with smartphone applications such as e-mail, an address book and a calendar to support teleworkers and employees in the field, ensuring that they have the most up-to-date information. By taking this approach, government agencies that already use smartphones and enterprise applications will only need basic training and incremental IT infrastructure changes.24 Mobile access can increase into other applications, including enterprise resource planning and public security systems. Of course, mobile capabilities will continue to be dependent upon available bandwidth and device requirements such as screen size.

In the area of unified communications, desk phone features will be built into smartphones, with mobile calls routed through the private branch exchange (PBX), which will extend organizations' voice policies to mobile calls. This approach helps ensure compliance with legal requirements such as maintaining call records and least-cost routing and allows organizations to own mobile phone numbers. Other emerging unified communication features on smartphones include advanced conferencing features such as "get-me" functions that ring all phones at a scheduled conference time and group voice message distribution with polling features to register responses.

Assessment: Are we ready yet?

Mobile workforce programs require a holistic approach that considers people, process and technology requirements. Addressing the people aspect of a mobile workforce begins with determining the right work and the right worker. Once identified, supervisors need tools and techniques to manage remote employees and metrics to measure productivity. Initial and on-going background checks help protect sensitive information.

Finally, on-going oversight from a policy office or steering committee helps keep the program on track.

Early adopters agree that positions that work well in a mobile work arrangement share these characteristics:

- ☐ low face-to-face communication requirements;
- ☐ communication most often achieved by phone, e-mail or text;
- ☐ large amounts of time spent handling information with work activities such as processing, analyzing, reading, programming and telephoning;
- ☐ a minimal need for special equipment; and
- ☐ well-defined tasks and measurable work products.

When selecting the right workers for a mobile workforce program, early adopters agree that employees who will be the most successful share these characteristics:

- ☐ self-motivation and self-discipline;
- ☐ strong organizational and time management skills;
- ☐ comfort working alone;
- ☐ ability to work independently with minimal supervision and feedback;
- ☐ success in current position;
- ☐ familiarity with the organization's procedures and policies;
- ☐ understanding of the effect of their participation in the program on other employees;
- ☐ effective communication skills and ability to be a team player;
- ☐ access to a safe, comfortable remote worksite where it's easy to concentrate;
- ☐ establishment of the required level of security;
- ☐ ownership of the necessary office equipment if it is not provided by the organization;
- ☐ access to separate office telephone line and voice mail, if required; and
- ☐ a household that supports working from home or remotely.25

Addressing process aspects of a remote workforce include encouraging participation and overcoming fear of change. Many organizations initially pilot mobile working position-by-position so efforts are closely monitored and adjusted before made widely available. Security and privacy issues must be addressed. Establishing guidelines to protect confidential information and implementing controls to monitor and protect the transfer of sensitive information are good practices for both on-and-offsite operations. Restricting downloads and the use of peer-to-peer and unapproved applications is essential. Carefully managing the use of personal devices for work purposes is a necessity when organizations require employees to use their own equipment for telework.

An up-front assessment of the key aspects of a mobile workforce — people, process and technology — increases the program's potential for success.

- ☐ Management readiness — Do supervisors and managers understand the benefits, requirements and challenges of managing employees in a virtual environment? Are they ready to use innovative tools and techniques to measure productivity and outcomes instead of traditional line-of-sight management?
- ☐ Do they understand the effort necessary to encourage collaboration and team work?
- ☐ Virtual worker readiness — Does the potential employee have the characteristics of a successful mobile worker? Will he/she make the effort to stay connected to the work place?

Appendices

- ☐ Does the position have well-defined tasks and measurable work products? Can their work be interrupted if glitches occur, especially during initial implementation?
- ☐ Operational readiness — Have we assessed work processes to ensure they fit well into the mobile work program? Have we established metrics for each position that allow us to measure productivity, quality and retention? Do we have a mandatory training program for employees and supervisors? Should we first test it as a pilot, assessing and adjusting after a fixed period of time?
- ☐ Technology readiness — Do the systems provide virtual workers the level of access necessary to perform their work and communicate with their customers remotely? Have we addressed bandwidth and availability of network services, performance and reliability of systems to be accessed, security and protection of information and systems, equipment needs at the remote site and IT support issues?

Conclusions

Needs and capabilities are converging to propel smartphones into the forefront of mobile work devices. Preferences of the next generation of mobile and connected workforce, the need to reduce trips due to traffic congestion and environmental concerns, continuous improvements in capabilities and access, and proven security and connectivity ensure smartphones their place as a preferred mobile platform for public sector agencies, turning today's mobile vision into tomorrow's virtual reality.

Appendix 6.

Presidential Directive

THE WHITE HOUSE Office of the Press Secretary

For Immediate Release October 5, 2009

EXECUTIVE ORDER

FEDERAL LEADERSHIP IN ENVIRONMENTAL, ENERGY, AND ECONOMIC PERFORMANCE

By the authority vested in me as President by the Constitution and the laws of the United States of America, and to establish an integrated strategy towards sustainability in the Federal government and to make reduction of greenhouse gas emissions a priority for Federal agencies, it is hereby ordered as follows:

Section 1. Policy. In order to create a clean energy economy that will increase our Nation's prosperity, promote energy security, protect the interests of taxpayers, and safeguard the health of our environment, the Federal government must lead by example. It is therefore the policy of the United States that Federal agencies shall increase energy efficiency; measure, report, and reduce their greenhouse gas emissions from direct and indirect activities; conserve and protect water resources through efficiency, reuse, and storm water management; eliminate waste, recycle, and prevent pollution; leverage agency acquisitions to foster markets for sustainable technologies and environmentally preferable materials, products, and services; design, construct, maintain, and operate high-performance sustainable buildings in sustainable locations; strengthen the vitality and livability of the communities in which Federal facilities are located; and inform Federal employees about and involve them in the achievement of these goals.

It is further the policy of the United States that to achieve these goals and support their respective missions, agencies shall prioritize actions based on a full accounting of both economic and social benefits and costs and shall drive continuous improvement by annually evaluating performance, extending or expanding projects that have net benefits, and reassessing or discontinuing under-performing projects.

Finally, it is also the policy of the United States that agencies' efforts and outcomes in implementing this order shall be transparent and that agencies shall therefore disclose results associated with the actions taken pursuant to this order on publicly available Federal websites.

Sec. 2. Goals for Agencies. In implementing the policy set forth in section 1 of this order, and preparing and implementing the Strategic Sustainability Performance Plan called for in section 8 of this order, the head of each agency shall:

within 90 days of the date of this order, establish and report to the Chair of the Council on Environmental Quality (CEQ Chair) and the Director of the Office of Management and Budget(OMB Director) a percentage reduction target for agency-wide more reductions of scope 1 and 2 greenhouse gas emissions in absolute terms by fiscal year 2020, relative to a fiscal year 2008baseline of the agency's scope 1 and 2 greenhouse gas emissions. Where appropriate, the target shall exclude direct emissions from excluded vehicles and equipment and from electric power produced and sold commercially to other parties in the course of regular business. This target shall be subject to review and approval by the CEQ Chair in consultation with the OMB Director under section 5 of this order. In establishing the target, the agency head shall consider reductions associated with: (i) reducing energy intensity in agency buildings; (ii) increasing agency use of renewable energy and implementing renewable energy generation projects on agency property; and (iii) reducing the use of fossil fuels by: (A) using low greenhouse gas emitting vehicles including alternative fuel vehicles; (B) optimizing the number of vehicles in the agency fleet; and (C) reducing, if the agency operates a fleet of at least 20 motor vehicles, the agency fleet's total consumption of petroleum products by a minimum of2 percent annually through the end of fiscal year2020, relative to a baseline of fiscal year 2005; (b) within 240 days of the date of this order and concurrent with submission of the Strategic Sustainability Performance Plan as described in section 8 of this order, establish and report to the CEQ Chair and the OMB Director a percentage reduction target for reducing agency-wide scope 3greenhouse gas emissions in absolute terms by fiscal year 2020,relative to a fiscal year 2008 baseline of agency scope 3emissions. This target shall be subject to review and approval by the CEQ Chair in consultation with the OMB Director under section 5 of this order. In establishing the target, the agency head shall consider reductions associated with: (i) pursuing opportunities with vendors and contractors to address and incorporate incentives to reduce greenhouse gas emissions(such as changes to manufacturing, utility or delivery services, modes of transportation used, or other changes in supply chain activities); (ii) implementing strategies and accommodations for transit, travel, training, and conferencing that actively support lower-carbon commuting and travel by agency staff; (iii) greenhouse gas emission reductions associated with pursuing other relevant goals in this section; and (iv) developing and implementing innovative policies and practices to address scope 3 greenhouse gas emissions unique to agency operations;

Appendices

(c) establish and report to the CEQ Chair and OMB Director a comprehensive inventory of absolute greenhouse gas emissions, including scope 1, scope 2, and specified scope 3 emissions(i) within 15 months of the date of this order for fiscal year 2010, and (ii) thereafter, annually at the end of January, for the preceding fiscal year. (d) improve water use efficiency and management by: (i) reducing potable water consumption intensity by2 percent annually through fiscal year 2020, or26 percent by the end of fiscal year 2020,relative to a baseline of the agency's water consumption in fiscal year 2007, by implementing water management strategies including water-efficient and low-flow fixtures and efficient cooling towers; (ii) reducing agency industrial, landscaping, and agricultural water consumption by 2 percent annually or 20 percent by the end of fiscal year 2020 relative to a baseline of the agency's industrial, landscaping, and agricultural water consumption in fiscal year2010; (iii) consistent with State law, identifying, promoting, and implementing water reuse strategies that reduce potable water consumption; and (iv) implementing and achieving the objectives identified in the storm water management guidance referenced in section 14 of this order; (e) promote pollution prevention and eliminate waste by: (i) minimizing the generation of waste and pollutants through source reduction; (ii) diverting at least 50 percent of non-hazardous solid waste, excluding construction and demolition debris, by the end of fiscal year2015; (iii) diverting at least 50 percent of construction and demolition materials and debris by the end of fiscal year 2015; (iv) reducing printing paper use and acquiring uncoated printing and writing paper containing at least 30 percent postconsumer fiber; (v) reducing and minimizing the quantity of toxic and hazardous chemicals and materials acquired, used, or disposed of; (vi) increasing diversion of compostable and organic material from the waste stream; (vii) implementing integrated pest management and other appropriate landscape management practices; more (viii) increasing agency use of acceptable alternative chemicals and processes in keeping with the agency's procurement policies; (ix) decreasing agency use of chemicals where such decrease will assist the agency in achieving greenhouse gas emission reduction targets under section 2(a) and (b) of this order; and (x) reporting in accordance with the requirements of sections 301 through 313 of the Emergency Planning and Community Right-to-Know Act of1986 (42 U.S.C. 11001 et seq.); (f) advance regional and local integrated planning by: (i) participating in regional transportation planning and recognizing existing community transportation infrastructure; (ii) aligning Federal policies to increase the effectiveness of local planning for energy choices such as locally generated renewable energy; (iii) ensuring that planning for new Federal facilities or new leases includes consideration of sites that are pedestrian friendly, near existing employment centers, and accessible to public transit, and emphasizes existing central cities and, in rural communities, existing or planned town centers; (iv) identifying and analyzing impacts from energy usage and alternative energy sources in all Environmental Impact Statements and Environmental Assessments for proposals for new or expanded Federal facilities under the National Environmental Policy Act of 1969, as amended (42 U.S.C. 4321 et seq.); and (v) coordinating with regional programs for Federal, State, tribal, and local ecosystem, watershed, and environmental management; (g) implement high performance sustainable Federal building design, construction, operation and management, maintenance, and deconstruction including by: (i) beginning in 2020 and thereafter, ensuring that all new Federal buildings that enter the planning process are designed to achieve zero-net-energy by 2030; (ii) ensuring that all new construction, major renovation, or repair and alteration of Federal buildings complies with the Guiding Principles for Federal Leadership in High Performance and Sustainable Buildings (Guiding Principles); (iii) ensuring that at least 15 percent of the agency's existing buildings (above 5,000 gross square feet) and building leases (above 5,000 gross square feet) meet the Guiding Principles by fiscal year 2015 and that the agency makes annual progress toward 100-percent conformance with the Guiding Principles for its building inventory; (iv) pursuing cost-effective, innovative strategies, such as highly reflective and vegetated roofs, to minimize consumption of energy, water, and materials; (v) managing existing building systems to reduce the consumption of energy, water, and materials, and identifying alternatives to renovation that reduce existing assets 'deferred maintenance costs; (vi) when adding assets to the agency's real property inventory, identifying opportunities to consolidate and dispose of existing assets, optimize the performance of the agency's real-property portfolio, and reduce associated environmental impacts; and (vii) ensuring that rehabilitation of Federally owned historic buildings utilizes best practices and technologies in retrofitting to promote long-term viability of the buildings; (h) advance sustainable acquisition to ensure that 95 percent of new contract actions including task and delivery orders, for products and services with the exception of acquisition of weapon systems, are energy-efficient (Energy Star or Federal Energy Management Program (FEMP) designated), water-efficient, bio based, environmentally preferable (e.g., Electronic Product Environmental Assessment Tool (EPEAT) certified), non-ozone depleting, contain recycled content, or are non-toxic or less-toxic alternatives, where such products and services meet agency performance requirements; (i) promote electronics stewardship, in particular by: (i) ensuring procurement preference for EPEAT-registered electronic products; (ii) establishing and implementing policies tenable power management, duplex printing, and other energy-efficient or environmentally preferable features on all eligible agency electronic products; (iii) employing environmentally sound practices with respect to the agency's disposition of all agency excess or surplus electronic products; (iv) ensuring the procurement of Energy Star and FEMP designated electronic equipment; (v) implementing best management practices for energy-efficient management of servers and Federal data centers; and (j) sustain environmental management, including by: (i) continuing implementation of formal environmental management systems at all appropriate organizational levels; and (ii) ensuring these formal systems are appropriately implemented and maintained to achieve the performance necessary to meet the goals of this order. Sec. 3. Steering Committee on Federal Sustainability. The OMB Director and the CEQ Chair shall: (a) establish an interagency Steering Committee (Steering Committee) on Federal Sustainability composed of the Federal Environmental Executive, designated under section 6 of Executive Order 13423 of January 24, 2007, and Agency Senior Sustainability Officers, designated under section 7 of this

Appendices

order, and that shall: (i) serve in the dual capacity of the Steering Committee on Strengthening Federal Environmental, Energy, and Transportation Management designated by the CEQ Chair pursuant to section 4 of Executive Order 13423; (ii) advise the OMB Director and the CEQ Chair on implementation of this order; (iii) facilitate the implementation of each agency's Strategic Sustainability Performance Plan; and (iv) share information and promote progress towards the goals of this order; (b) enlist the support of other organizations within the Federal government to assist the Steering Committee in addressing the goals of this order; (c) establish and disband, as appropriate, interagency subcommittees of the Steering Committee, to assist the Steering Committee in carrying out its responsibilities; (d) determine appropriate Federal actions to achieve the policy of section 1 and the goals of section 2 of this order; (e) ensure that Federal agencies are held accountable for conformance with the requirements of this order; and (f) in coordination with the Department of Energy's Federal Energy Management Program and the Office of the Federal Environmental Executive designated under section 6 of executive Order 13423, provide guidance and assistance to facilitate the development of agency targets for greenhouse gas emission reductions required under subsections 2(a) and (b) of this order. Sec. 4. Additional Duties of the Director of the Office of Management and Budget. In addition to the duties of the OMB Director specified elsewhere in this order, the OMB Director shall: (a) review and approve each agency's multi-year Strategic Sustainability Performance Plan under section 8 of this order and each update of the Plan. The Director shall, where feasible, review each agency's Plan concurrently with OMB's review and evaluation of the agency's budget request; (b) prepare scorecards providing periodic evaluation of Federal agency performance in implementing this order and publish scorecard results on a publicly available website; and (c) approve and issue instructions to the heads of agencies concerning budget and appropriations matters relating to implementation of this order.

Sec. 5. Additional Duties of the Chair of the Council on Environmental Quality. In addition to the duties of the CEQ Chair specified elsewhere in this order, the CEQ Chair shall:

(a) issue guidance for greenhouse gas accounting and reporting required under section 2 of this order;

(b) issue instructions to implement this order, in addition to instructions within the authority of the OMB Director to issue under subsection 4(c) of this order;

(c) review and approve each agency's targets, in consultation with the OMB Director, for agency-wide reductions of greenhouse gas emissions under section 2 of this order;

(d) prepare, in coordination with the OMB Director, streamlined reporting metrics to determine each agency's progress under section 2 of this order;

(e) review and evaluate each agency's multi-year Strategic Sustainability Performance Plan under section 8 of this order and each update of the Plan;

(f) assess agency progress toward achieving the goals and policies of this order, and provide its assessment of the agency's progress to the OMB Director;

(g) within 120 days of the date of this order, provide the President with an aggregate Federal government-wide target for reducing scope 1 and 2 greenhouse gas emissions in absolute terms by fiscal year 2020 relative to a fiscal year 2008 baseline;

(h) within 270 days of the date of this order, provide the President with an aggregate Federal government-wide target for reducing scope 3 greenhouse gas emissions in absolute terms by fiscal year 2020 relative to a fiscal year 2008 baseline;

(i) establish and disband, as appropriate, interagency working groups to provide recommendations to the CEQ for areas of Federal agency operational and managerial improvement associated with the goals of this order; and

(j) administer the Presidential leadership awards program, established under subsection 4(c) of Executive Order 13423, to recognize exceptional and outstanding agency performance with respect to achieving the goals of this order and to recognize extraordinary innovation, technologies, and practices employed to achieve the goals of this order.

Sec. 6. Duties of the Federal Environmental Executive. The Federal Environmental Executive designated by the President to head the Office of the Federal Environmental Executive, pursuant to section 6 of Executive Order 13423, shall: (a) identify strategies and tools to assist Federal implementation efforts under this order, including through the sharing of best practices from successful Federal sustainability efforts; and (b) monitor and advise the CEQ Chair and the OMB Director on the agencies' implementation of this order and their progress in achieving the orders policies and goals.

Sec. 7. Agency Senior Sustainability Officers. (a) Within 30 days of the date of this order, the head of each agency shall designate from among the agency's senior management officials a Senior Sustainability Officer who shall be accountable for agency conformance with the requirements of this order; and shall report such designation to the OMB Director and the CEQ Chair. (b) The Senior Sustainability Officer for each agency shall perform the functions of the senior agency official designated by the head of each agency pursuant to section 3(d)(i) of executive Order 13423 and shall be responsible for: (i) preparing the targets for agency-wide reductions and the inventory of greenhouse gas emissions required under subsections 2(a), (b), and (c) of this order; (ii) within 240 days of the date of this order, and annually thereafter, preparing and submitting to the CEQ Chair and the OMB Director, for their review and approval, a multi-year Strategic Sustainability Performance Plan (Sustainability Plan or Plan) as described in section 8 of this order; (iii) preparing and implementing the approved Plan in coordination with appropriate offices and organizations within the agency including the General Counsel, Chief Information Officer, Chief Acquisition

Appendices

Officer, Chief Financial Officer, and Senior Real Property Officers, and in coordination with other agency plans, policies, and activities; (iv) monitoring the agency's performance and progress in implementing the Plan, and reporting the performance and progress to the CEQ Chair and the OMB Director, on such schedule and in such format as the Chair and the Director may require; and (v) reporting annually to the head of the agency on the adequacy and effectiveness of the agency's Plan in implementing this order. Sec. 8. Agency Strategic Sustainability Performance Plan. Each agency shall develop, implement, and annually update an integrated Strategic Sustainability Performance Plan that will prioritize agency actions based on lifecycle on investment. Each agency Plan and update shall be subject to approval by the OMB Director under section 4 of this order. With respect to the period beginning in fiscal year 2011 and continuing through the end of fiscal year 2021, each agency Plan shall:

(a) include a policy statement committing the agency to compliance with environmental and energy statutes, regulations, and Executive Orders;

(b) achieve the sustainability goals and targets, including greenhouse gas reduction targets, established under section 2 of this order;

(c) be integrated into the agency's strategic planning and budget process, including the agency's strategic plan under section 3 of the Government Performance and Results Act of 1993, as amended (5 U.S.C. 306);

(d) identify agency activities, policies, plans, procedures, and practices that are relevant to the agency's implementation of this order, and where necessary, provide for development and implementation of new or revised policies, plans, procedures, and practices;

(e) identify specific agency goals, a schedule, milestones, and approaches for achieving results, and quantifiable metrics for agency implementation of this order;

(f) take into consideration environmental measures as well as economic and social benefits and costs in evaluating projects and activities based on lifecycle return on investment;

(g) outline planned actions to provide information about agency progress and performance with respect to achieving the goals of this order on a publicly available Federal website;

(h) incorporate actions for achieving progress metrics identified by the OMB Director and the CEQ Chair;

(i) evaluate agency climate-change risks and vulnerabilities to manage the effects of climate change on the agency's operations and mission in both the short and long term; and

(j) identify in annual updates opportunities for improvement and evaluation of past performance in order to extend or expand projects that have net lifecycle benefits, and reassess or discontinue under-performing projects.

Sec. 9. Recommendations for Greenhouse Gas Accounting and Reporting. The Department of Energy, through its Federal Energy Management Program, and in coordination with the Environmental Protection Agency, the Department of Defense, the General Services Administration, the Department of the Interior, the Department of Commerce, and other agencies as appropriate, shall:

(a) within 180 days of the date of this order develop and provide to the CEQ Chair recommended Federal greenhouse gas reporting and accounting procedures for agencies to use in carrying out their obligations under subsections 2(a), (b), and

(c) of this order, including procedures that will ensure that agencies: (i) accurately and consistently quantify and account for greenhouse gas emissions from all scope 1, 2, and 3 sources, using accepted greenhouse gas accounting and reporting principles, and identify appropriate opportunities to revise the fiscal year 2008 baseline to address significant changes in factors affecting agency emissions such as reorganization and improvements in accuracy of data collection and estimation procedures or other major changes that would otherwise render the initial baseline information unsuitable; (ii) consider past Federal agency efforts to reduce greenhouse gas emissions; and (iii) consider and account for sequestration and emissions of greenhouse gases resulting from Federal land management practices; (b) within 1 year of the date of this order, to ensure consistent and accurate reporting under this section, provide electronic accounting and reporting capability for the Federal greenhouse gas reporting procedures developed under subsection (a) of this section, and to the extent practicable, ensure compatibility between this capability and existing Federal agency reporting systems; and (c) every 3 years from the date of the CEQ Chair's issuance of the initial version of the reporting guidance, and as otherwise necessary, develop and provide recommendations to the CEQ Chair for revised Federal greenhouse gas reporting procedures for agencies to use in implementing subsections 2(a), (b), and (c) of this order.

Sec. 10. Recommendations for Sustainable Locations for Federal Facilities. Within 180 days of the date of this order, the Department of Transportation, in accordance with its Sustainable Partnership Agreement with the Department of Housing and Urban Development and the Environmental Protection Agency, and in coordination with the General Services Administration, the Department of Homeland Security, the Department of Defense, and other agencies as appropriate, shall: (a) review existing policies and practices associated with site selection for Federal facilities; and (b) provide recommendations to the CEQ Chair regarding sustainable location strategies for consideration in Sustainability Plans. The recommendations shall be consistent with principles of sustainable development including prioritizing central business district and rural town center locations, prioritizing sites well served by transit, including site design elements that ensure safe and convenient pedestrian access, consideration of transit access and proximity to housing affordable to a wide range of Federal employees, adaptive reuse or renovation of buildings, avoidance of development of sensitive land resources, and evaluation of parking management strategies.

Sec. 11. Recommendations for Federal Local Transportation Logistics. Within 180 days of the date of this order, the General Services Administration, in coordination with the Department of Transportation, the Department of the Treasury, the Department of Energy, the Office of Personnel Management, and other agencies as appropriate, shall review current policies and practices associated with use of public transportation by Federal personnel, Federal shuttle bus and vehicle transportation routes supported by multiple Federal agencies, and use of alternative fuel vehicles in Federal shuttle bus fleets, and shall provide recommendations to the CEQ Chair on how these policies and practices could be revised to support the implementation of this order and the achievement of its policies and goals. Sec. 12. Guidance for Federal Fleet Management. Within 180 days of the date of this order, the Department of Energy, in coordination with the General Services Administration, shall issue guidance on Federal fleet management that addresses the acquisition of alternative fuel vehicles and use of alternative fuels; the use of biodiesel blends in diesel vehicles; the acquisition of electric vehicles for appropriate functions; improvement of fleet fuel economy; the optimizing of fleets to the agency mission; petroleum reduction strategies, such as the acquisition of low greenhouse gas emitting vehicles and the reduction of vehicle miles traveled; and the installation of renewable fuel pumps at Federal fleet fueling centers.

Sec. 13. Recommendations for Vendor and Contractor Emissions. Within 180 days of the date of this order, the General Services Administration, in coordination with the Department of Defense, the Environmental Protection Agency, and other agencies as appropriate, shall review and provide recommendations to the CEQ Chair and the Administrator of OMB's Office of Federal Procurement Policy regarding the feasibility of working with the Federal vendor and contractor community to provide information that will assist Federal agencies in tracking and reducing scope 3 greenhouse gas emissions related to the supply of products and services to the Government. These recommendations should consider the potential impacts on the procurement process, and the Federal vendor and contractor community including small businesses and other socioeconomic procurement programs. Recommendations should also explore the feasibility of: (a) requiring vendors and contractors to register with a voluntary registry or organization for reporting greenhouse gas emissions; (b) requiring contractors, as part of a new or revised registration under the Central Contractor Registration or other tracking system, to develop and make available its greenhouse gas inventory and description of efforts to mitigate greenhouse gas emissions; (c) using Federal government purchasing preferences or other incentives for products manufactured using processes that minimize greenhouse gas emissions; and (d) other options for encouraging sustainable practices and reducing greenhouse gas emissions.

Sec. 14. Storm water Guidance for Federal Facilities. Within 60 days of the date of this order, the Environmental Protection Agency, in coordination with other Federal agencies as appropriate, shall issue guidance on the implementation of section 438 of the Energy Independence and Security Act of 2007(42 U.S.C. 17094).

Sec. 15. Regional Coordination. Within 180 days of the date of this order, the Federal Environmental Executive shall develop and implement a regional implementation plan to support the goals of this order taking into account energy and environmental priorities of particular regions of the United States.

Sec. 16. Agency Roles in Support of Federal Adaptation Strategy. In addition to other roles and responsibilities of agencies with respect to environmental leadership as specified in this order, the agencies shall participate actively in the interagency Climate Change Adaptation Task Force, which is already engaged in developing the domestic and international dimensions of a U.S. strategy for adaptation to climate change, and shall develop approaches through which the policies and practices of the agencies can be made compatible with and reinforce that strategy. Within 1 year of the date of this order the CEQ Chair shall provide to the President, following consultation with the agencies and the Climate Change Adaptation Task Force, as appropriate, a progress report on agency actions in support of the national adaptation strategy and recommendations for any further such measures as the CEQ Chair may deem necessary.

Sec. 17. Limitations. (a) This order shall apply to an agency with respect to the activities, personnel, resources, and facilities of the agency that are located within the United States. The head of an agency may provide that this order shall apply in whole or in part with respect to the activities, personnel, resources, and facilities of the agency that are not located within the United States, if the head of the agency determines that such application is in the interest of the United States. (b) The head of an agency shall manage activities, personnel, resources, and facilities of the agency that are not located within the United States, and with respect to which the head of the agency has not made a determination under subsection (a) of this section, in a manner consistent with the policy set forth in section 1 of this order to the extent the head of the agency determines practicable.

Sec. 18. Exemption Authority. (a) The Director of National Intelligence may exempt an intelligence activity of the United States, and related personnel, resources, and facilities, from the provisions of this order, other than this subsection and section 20, to the extent the Director determines necessary to protect intelligence sources and methods from unauthorized disclosure. (b) The head of an agency may exempt law enforcement activities of that agency, and related

Appendices

personnel, resources, and facilities, from the provisions of this order, other than this subsection and section 20, to the extent the head of an agency determines necessary to protect undercover operations from unauthorized disclosure. (c) (i) The head of an agency may exempt law enforcement, protective, emergency response, or military tactical vehicle fleets of that agency from the provisions of this order, other than this subsection and section 20. 12 more 13 (ii) Heads of agencies shall manage fleets to which paragraph (i) of this subsection refers in a manner consistent with the policy set forth in section 1 of this order to the extent they determine practicable. (d) The head of an agency may exempt particular agency activities and facilities from the provisions of this order, other than this subsection and section 20, where it is in the interest of national security. If the head of an agency issues an exemption under this section, the agency must notify the CEQ Chair in writing within 30 days of issuance of the exemption under this subsection. To the maximum extent practicable, and without compromising national security, each agency shall strive to comply with the purposes, goals, and implementation steps in this order. (e) The head of an agency may submit to the President, through the CEQ Chair, a request for an exemption of an agency activity, and related personnel, resources, and facilities, from this order.

Sec. 19. Definitions. As used in this order: (a) "absolute greenhouse gas emissions" means total greenhouse gas emissions without normalization for activity levels and includes any allowable consideration of sequestration; (b) "agency" means an executive agency as defined in section 105 of title 5, United States Code, excluding the Government Accountability Office; (c) "alternative fuel vehicle" means vehicles defined by section 301 of the Energy Policy Act of 1992, as amended (42 U.S.C. 13211), and otherwise includes electric fueled vehicles, hybrid electric vehicles, plug-in hybrid electric vehicles, dedicated alternative fuel vehicles, dual fueled alternative fuel vehicles, qualified fuel cell motor vehicles, advanced lean burn technology motor vehicles, self-propelled vehicles such as bicycles and any other alternative fuel vehicles that are defined by statute; (d) "construction and demolition materials and debris" means materials and debris generated during construction, renovation, demolition, or dismantling of all structures and buildings and associated infrastructure; (e) "divert" and "diverting" means redirecting materials that might otherwise be placed in the waste stream to recycling or recovery, excluding diversion to waste-to-energy facilities; (f) "energy intensity" means energy consumption per square foot of building space, including industrial or laboratory facilities; (g) "environmental" means environmental aspects of internal agency operations and activities, including those aspects related to energy and transportation functions; (h) "excluded vehicles and equipment" means any vehicle, vessel, aircraft, or non-road equipment owned or operated by an agency of the that is used in: more (i) combat support, combat service support, tactical or relief operations, or training for such operations; (ii) Federal law enforcement (including protective service and investigation); (iii) emergency response (including fire and rescue);or (iv) spaceflight vehicles (including associated ground-support equipment); (i) "greenhouse gases" means carbon dioxide, methane, nitrous oxide, hydrofluorocarbons, perfluorocarbons, and sulfurhexafluoride; (j) "renewable energy" means energy produced by solar, wind, biomass, landfill gas, ocean (including tidal, wave, current, and thermal), geothermal, municipal solid waste, or new hydroelectric generation capacity achieved from increased efficiency or additions of new capacity at an existing hydroelectric project; (k) "scope 1, 2, and 3" mean; (i) scope 1: direct greenhouse gas emissions from sources that are owned or controlled by the Federal agency; (ii) scope 2: direct greenhouse gas emissions resulting from the generation of electricity, heat, or steam purchased by a Federal agency; and (iii) scope 3: greenhouse gas emissions from sources not owned or directly controlled by a Federal agency but related to agency activities such as vendor supply chains, delivery services, and employee travel and commuting; (l) "sustainability" and "sustainable" mean to create and maintain conditions, under which humans and nature can exist in productive harmony, that permit fulfilling the social, economic, and other requirements of present and future generations; (m) "United States" means the fifty States, the District of Columbia, the Commonwealth of Puerto Rico, Guam, American Samoa, the United States Virgin Islands, and the Northern Mariana Islands, and associated territorial waters and airspace; (n) "water consumption intensity" means water consumption per square foot of building space; and (o) "zero-net-energy building" means a building that is designed, constructed, and operated to require a greatly reduced quantity of energy to operate, meet the balance of energy needs from sources of energy that do not produce greenhouse gases, and therefore result in no net emissions of greenhouse gases and be economically viable.

Sec. 20. General Provisions. (a) This order shall be implemented in a manner consistent with applicable law and subject to the availability of appropriations.

(b) Nothing in this order shall be construed to impair or otherwise affect the functions of the OMB Director relating to budgetary, administrative, or legislative proposals.

(c) This order is intended only to improve the internal management of the Federal government and is not intended to, and does not, create any right or benefit, substantive or procedural, enforceable at law or in equity by any party against the United States, its departments, agencies, or entities, its officers, employees, or agents, or any other person.

BARACK OBAMA

THE WHITE HOUSE, October 5, 2009.